STEPHEN BERESFORD

Stephen Beresford trained at RADA and worked as an actor before writing for television and film. *The Last of the Haussmans* is his first play. Current work includes a second play for the National Theatre, a feature film for Pathé and three separate projects for NBC Universal.

As an actor, theatre credits include *Free*, *She Stoops to Conquer*, *A Laughing Matter* (National Theatre); *Woyzeck* (Gate Theatre, directed by Sarah Kane); *Shopping and Fucking* and *Our Country's Good* (Out of Joint, directed by Max Stafford-Clark).

Other Titles in this Series

Stephen Beresford

THE LAST OF THE HAUSSMANS

NICK HERN BOOKS
London
www.nickhernbooks.co.uk

A Nick Hern Book

The Last of the Haussmans first published in Great Britain in 2012 as a paperback original by Nick Hern Books Limited, 14 Larden Road, London W3 7ST

The Last of the Haussmans copyright © 2012 Stephen Beresford

Stephen Beresford has asserted his right to be identified as the author of this work

Cover image: photo by Phil Fisk (copyright © philfisk.com), taken from the original National Theatre poster, designed by Charlotte Wilkinson
Cover design: Ned Hoste, 2H

Typeset by Nick Hern Books, London
Printed in the UK by CPI Group (UK) Ltd

ISBN 978 1 84842 252 0

A CIP catalogue record for this book is available from the British Library

For J.M. Lewthwaite

The Last of the Haussmans was first performed in the Lyttelton auditorium of the National Theatre, London, on 19 June 2012 (previews from 12 June), with the following cast:

DANIEL	Taron Egerton
NICK	Rory Kinnear
SUMMER	Isabella Laughland
LIBBY	Helen McCrory
PETER	Matthew Marsh
JUDY	Julie Walters

Director	Howard Davies
Designer	Vicki Mortimer
Lighting Designer	Mark Henderson
Sound Designer	Christopher Shutt
Projection Designer	Jon Driscoll

Characters

LIBBY, *forties*
NICK, *late thirties*
SUMMER, *fifteen*
JUDY, *sixties*
DANIEL, *nineteen*
PETER, *fifties*

*A forward slash (/) in the text indicates the point at which the next
speaker interrupts.*

*This text went to press before the end of rehearsals and so may
differ slightly from the play as performed.*

ACT ONE

Summer

Scene One

*The garden and sun terrace of the Haussman family home on
the South Devon coast. The house is a 1930's art deco property
in a state of virtual dereliction. The overgrown garden and
terrace are littered with furniture – some of it garden furniture,
some of it not – and the solarium, a glass room attached to the
house with tall glass doors, is also piled high with junk. There is
a large poster in the solarium of a charismatic, dark-eyed
Indian man with a huge silver beard. This is the Bhagwan Shree
Rajneesh. A woman, LIBBY, stands in the garden, smoking.
Facing her is a man, NICK. He's unshaven and unkempt with
nicotine-stained fingers, almost like a tramp – but with a faint
air of the exotic about him.*

LIBBY. I know you haven't been looking after yourself because
  your nail varnish is chipped. And you're incredibly thin.

NICK. I've always been thin.

LIBBY. Not like that.

  Beat.

  Hello, anyway.

NICK. Hello.

LIBBY. Do you want something to eat? I don't know what there
  is. Ritz Crackers? For some reason she's got boxes of the
  things. '

NICK. Really, I'm fine.

LIBBY. Or quiche.

NICK. I'm alright actually, Libby. Thank you. I'll just have a drink please. Dying for a drink.

LIBBY *goes to fetch a glass.*

Where is she?

LIBBY. Upstairs.

NICK. Am I – ? Do I have to go up?

LIBBY. You'd never wake her anyway. She sleeps all day and gets up when she's hungry. She's like a fucking badger.

NICK. Is she – ? I mean – Do I have to prepare myself?

LIBBY. What do you mean?

NICK. For the – I mean – is she changed?

LIBBY. Jesus, Nick, you're not going to get stupid about this, are you? She had a melanoma so small it was removed with a local anaesthetic. Okay?

NICK. Alright.

LIBBY. It's not *Terms of Endearment.*

LIBBY *hands him a glass. Pause.*

I had a lot of trouble tracking you down this time. None of the numbers I had for you worked. I was worried.

NICK. Don't be.

LIBBY. I spoke to who knows how many people.

NICK. I move around.

LIBBY. Someone said you'd left your job.

NICK. Who?

LIBBY. I don't know. Chris or something. Tim.

NICK. Rory?

LIBBY. I don't know. Everyone passed me on to someone else. I got the impression you were sleeping on floors. I rang that

guy in the end. What was his name? The one that you –
Sandy? I never knew if you two were lovers. Or –

NICK. We weren't. Exactly.

LIBBY. He told me you'd gone to Corfu.

NICK. I was living in this awful place, Lib. The people were –
Somebody was trying to kill me. Seriously. This guy who
was a friend of Sandy's flatmate was actually threatening to
kill me.

LIBBY. Why?

NICK. With a circular saw.

LIBBY. Why, I said. Not how.

NICK. Oh. Nothing. Housing benefit. And I'd heard about this
amazing sort of beach community in Corfu. It sounded so
wonderful. Just surrounded by sea and sky and space. So I
fucked off.

LIBBY. To Corfu?

NICK. To Bristol. I couldn't quite raise the funds for Corfu. But
I had a friend in Bristol. Lois. Remember her? She lost her
leg. She was in my recovery programme. Lois. The Quaker.

Beat.

Quaker now. Used to be a glue-sniffer. Anyway. That's –
How long have you been here?

LIBBY. Couple of weeks.

NICK. And what's she like? I mean, apart from –

LIBBY. The same. Madder.

She suddenly stops.

She's writing her memoirs.

NICK. Her what?

LIBBY. She's writing a fucking book.

LIBBY *has picked up a Dictaphone. She presses play. We hear* JUDY*'s voice.*

JUDY (*on Dictaphone*). All one hundred and thirty-seven Sanskrit verses of the Guru Gita.

LIBBY. She's – listen.

Fast-forward. Play.

JUDY (*on Dictaphone*). And you open like a flower…

LIBBY. Hang on a minute.

Fast-forward again, impatiently.

JUDY (*on Dictaphone*). Rice noodles…

Fast-forward again.

The spitting image of Burt Reynolds.

NICK. Does it matter?

LIBBY. Of course it matters. Do you want her version of events floating around out there? Unchallenged?

NICK. They wouldn't publish it.

LIBBY. You'd be surprised what they'd publish. She sits here, night after night, dictating it to – and this is the other thing – her new best friend.

NICK. Who?

LIBBY. This doctor.

NICK. Dr Mays?

LIBBY. No – *Dr Mays*? Dr Mays is dead.

NICK. Is he?

LIBBY. Of course. What did you think he was going to do? Limp on for ever? This is the new GP. Only, he's an old hippy, isn't he? Sits here and drinks with her, night after night. Plays the guitar. How that can be good for her, Joan Baez and Bob fucking Dylan till three in the morning. And you should see the way he looks at me.

NICK. Oh?

LIBBY. Jesus Christ. I don't know why I attract these old men.

Little pause.

She'll be down in a minute.

NICK. What exactly happened?

LIBBY. What do you mean?

NICK. With the – raid – Is that what we call it?

LIBBY. It isn't funny. What made it worse, the health visitor was Jackie Miller.

NICK. Who?

LIBBY. Her mother used to clean here. Couldn't wait to get over the threshold. Dear me, she kept saying. It's been very difficult to cope, hasn't it? Eyes on stalks.

NICK. Jesus, I'm nervous.

LIBBY. Why?

NICK. Perhaps I'll have another.

LIBBY. We've got three months. And then we get another check. They want to see significant improvements. I told them, it's not going to happen overnight. But we need to do this, Nick. For us. I mean, this cancer has really brought it home to me. We could – Well. There's no reason why we shouldn't –

Beat.

I don't know about you, but I'm sick of wandering around without a proper home.

SUMMER *has walked out.*

You remember Summer.

NICK. What? Summer? That can't be Summer.

SUMMER. I'm pretty sure it is.

NICK. But she's –

LIBBY. Fifteen.

(*To* SUMMER.) Are you hungry? I'm the only person in this house who eats. I'm going to wake her in a minute. This is ridiculous.

LIBBY *disappears*.

NICK. Do you know who I am? I'm Nick. I'm your Uncle Nick.

SUMMER. I know.

NICK. I remember you as a very little girl.

SUMMER. Right.

NICK. A very tiny little girl.

SUMMER. Yeah. That's how we start out.

NICK *gets another drink*.

NICK. So… Are you…?

SUMMER. What did my mum say to you?

NICK. What?

SUMMER. About me? Did she slag me off?

NICK. No.

SUMMER. She's got a lot of anger, don't you think?

NICK. Your mum?

SUMMER. She carries it. Have you ever tried living with someone like that?

NICK. Yes. Yes. I have, as a matter of fact. He was a roofer.

To tell you the truth, I'm quite frightened of her.

SUMMER. She's frightened of you.

NICK. Don't be ridiculous.

SUMMER. She is. She's frightened you'll get back on the smack.

NICK. What do you know about that?

SUMMER. I can remember it. When they found you in that flat and Mum brought you back here. I was six. You had to be carried upstairs. They fed you Ready brek. I did it once. It was the only thing you could keep down. You can remember a lot from the age of six.

NICK. Yes. Yes, you can.

Beat. SUMMER *looks at the poster.*

SUMMER. That guy.

NICK. Bhagwan.

SUMMER. Yeah. Bhagwan. He's the one, isn't he? The cult. He had fourteen Rolls Royces.

NICK. More, I should think. It wasn't a cult. Not really.

SUMMER. They were all boning each other.

NICK. Yes. That much is true. They were. All boning each other.

SUMMER. I think she's alright.

NICK. Judy?

SUMMER. Bit of a fucking hippy, but – Don't you?

NICK. Well. I –

SUMMER. Don't lie. Just because she's had cancer.

NICK. I feel – I feel the same way about her as you do about your mother. I expect.

SUMMER. That whore. She wants me to go to my dad's.

NICK. Ah.

SUMMER. For the whole summer.

NICK. I didn't know your dad was on the scene.

SUMMER. He wasn't. This is a new development. Why the fuck should I get farmed off on a total stranger so that she can get up to who the fuck knows what down here? It's bullshit. Have you ever met him?

NICK. No.

SUMMER. Neither have I. I'm not going. He's old, isn't he?

NICK. Quite old. Older than your mum.

SUMMER. I was a mistake. Skiing holiday.

NICK. I know.

SUMMER. They didn't even have a relationship. Stupid cow. And what the fuck she was doing on a skiing holiday is beyond me. Normally all she wants to do is lie on her arse and read *Grazia*. Lazy bitch. Are you gay?

NICK *nods*.

I'm bisexual.

NICK. You mustn't be too hard on your mum. This – All this – It's very stressful. Coming here. Dealing with Judy.

SUMMER. Is that what she told you? That she came here to deal with Judy?

NICK. That's why we're all here. Isn't it? The clean-up?

SUMMER. We're here because she got dumped.

NICK. What?

SUMMER. Roy. The bracelet-wearer. She needed somewhere to lick her wounds, didn't she? This is what she always does. Run away. Can you imagine having sex with a man who wears chunky bracelets?

NICK. You'd be surprised the things I can imagine.

SUMMER. She's got no class. I could have told her he wasn't going to stick around. Why should he? She gave him everything he was after in the first three nights. They had sex in a golf cart.

LIBBY *appears*.

LIBBY. She's getting up.

NICK. Libby –

LIBBY. Why don't you take Nick's bags upstairs.

NICK. Do you mind if I – I'm just a bit worried about how long all this is going to take.

LIBBY. What?

NICK. This. All this.

LIBBY. What do you mean, worried?

NICK. Well, I – I do have a sort of a – a commitment.

LIBBY. What?

NICK. I'm sort of expected somewhere.

LIBBY. I don't believe this.

NICK. I'd come straight back –

LIBBY. No. NO. This is one time you are not leaving me with all the shit. Jesus Christ! Are you – ? Do you seriously think you can creep off again and leave it all to me? Summer, go upstairs. I am exhausted, Nicky –

NICK. Forget it, Lib –

LIBBY. I am sick and tired of it. All of it.

NICK. I know. Forget it. I didn't mean it.

LIBBY. Summer –

SUMMER. Yeah, like I'm missing this.

NICK. I am absolutely not – I'm sorry. It was an error – I'm sorry. Libby, please – I won't leave you. I won't. I promise.

JUDY (*off*). Libby?

NICK. I think it was probably just a reaction. I'm – I just – I'm a bit tense – She makes me tense.

LIBBY. Just breathe.

NICK. Even her voice –

LIBBY. Look at me.

JUDY (*off*). Lib – ?

LIBBY. We're outside!

> SUMMER *takes* NICK*'s bag inside. After a second, we see* JUDY. *She has long silver hair which is wild and unkempt and is wearing a very stained and rather incongruous Snoopy nightdress. She enters the garden. A little silence.*

JUDY. Well.

NICK. Hello, Mum.

JUDY. Oh, Libby. Look. Isn't he beautiful?

LIBBY. He's very thin.

JUDY. That's just his frame – Nijinsky. When did you arrive?

LIBBY. Just now.

JUDY. I'm in an absolute daze. Look at me.

LIBBY. You could've got dressed, Mum.

JUDY. Snoopy. I live in these tops. Tell me everything, Nick. I want to know. Are you well? He looks like my mother.

LIBBY. What?

JUDY. He has my mother's beauty. Don't you think? Her beautiful face.

LIBBY. He needs to look after himself.

JUDY. What for? He's invincible like his old mum. What do you do, Nicky? I want to know all about your work. Do you write?

NICK. No.

JUDY. You ought to be a writer. I've always said that.

NICK. Really?

JUDY. Fiction. I've been saying it for years.

LIBBY. I've never heard you.

JUDY. How can we celebrate? Oh, Nick, aren't you crazy about your niece?

NICK. Yes, I –

JUDY. She's an Apache. Absolutely wild. Look – three generations.

LIBBY. We need to make a decision about sleeping arrangements.

JUDY. Yes, in a minute, Libby.

NICK. How are you? I mean – Are you – ?

JUDY. Oh! I had to go to Plymouth to have a big chunk cut out of my leg, Nicky, and guess what that meant? An Indian doctor. I told him all about Poona and the ashram. Oh my God, he was beautiful, wasn't he, Libby?

LIBBY. I really don't know.

JUDY. Oh, he was. And when he put his hand on my thigh – you'll understand this, Nicky – I felt such a jolt go through me, I said, 'Kama wakens me with his arrow,' which I think was rather smart. Don't you? He just went quiet. Now. Listen – isn't there – There's a sort of a Christmas drink, what is it, Summer? Coconut.

SUMMER. Malibu.

JUDY. There's Malibu, Nick. Is that the sort of thing you'd like?

NICK. I'm perfectly happy with gin.

JUDY. Yes. Me too. Shall we eat something?

LIBBY. There's a bit of salad left.

JUDY. And some quiche. It's from the Spar, Nick, but I snip my own chives over it. Or crackers! There are these wonderful little crackers, Nick. I'm addicted to them.

LIBBY. Ritz.

JUDY. They're called Ritz, isn't that priceless? And they are, Nicky. They're exactly like something you'd have at the Ritz.

Beat.

Do you know, there was a little lark here this morning? While I was doing my exercises. I'd never seen him before.

He just hopped up onto this step and tipped about. I think it was a sign of your arrival. I see signs in everything.

JUDY *heads back towards the house.*

LIBBY. Nick, will you sleep in Grandpa's study?

JUDY (*stopping and turning*). We were raided, Nick.

NICK. I heard.

JUDY. It's all second homes here now. Fucking fascist pigs. They don't want me to drive down the value of their exclusive little bolt-holes. Well. I am.

LIBBY. Go indoors.

JUDY. This is property. Do you see? It's the greatest agent of control ever devised by any government anywhere. Get people to care about their property and you don't even have to police the state. They do it for you. Residents' association? They're worse than the Stasi.

(*After* SUMMER.) Summer, darling, put some music on.

She looks back at NICK.

Do you know, this is the nicest thing that's happened, Nick. You coming here.

She sets off into the house. Then –

And Libby.

LIBBY. There you are. Prodigal son. I don't know what you were worrying about –

NICK *lets out a little sob.*

Nick?

NICK. I'm sorry.

LIBBY. What's the matter?

NICK. It's just – I don't know. The shock, or something. And sickness. I fucking hate sickness. Oh God, and I'm sorry, Libby –

LIBBY. What for?

NICK. We always stuck together, Lib. Through all of it. Didn't we? What happened to us? To me?

LIBBY. Calm down. It's not that bad. It really isn't. You're just – You're tired.

NICK. Yes.

LIBBY. You're overwrought.

> LIBBY *offers him a drag of her cigarette, which he takes.*

Alright now?

He nods. Little pause.

NICK. Summer seems sweet.

LIBBY. Does she? Not when I'm around.

NICK. That's just her age.

LIBBY. She hates me, Nick.

NICK. No –

LIBBY. She does. I'm telling you. She's aggressive, rude. Moody. She never smiles. Anything less like Summer, it's hard to imagine.

NICK. They go through phases.

LIBBY. No. This – This is – And whatever she said to you, Nick, I suggest you take it with a pinch of salt. She's a notorious storyteller. She told them at school she was diabetic. I have no idea why.

NICK. Well. She's lively.

LIBBY. She's that alright.

NICK. And smart. Was I that sophisticated at fifteen?

LIBBY. You should see her with a full face of make-up. She could very easily pass for twenty-six. And does, I expect. No. She doesn't like me. Not one bit.

NICK. She said you'd had a bit of – That you'd been – Of course, this may have been –

LIBBY. Oh God, no. She doesn't need to fabricate my misfortunes. I had a – A relationship came to an end. He was – Well, I liked him. Stupid, really. You shouldn't get your heart broken at my age.

NICK. My heart is permanently being broken.

Music comes from inside. Indian music.

LIBBY. We'd better go in.

She gets up.

Eat our crackers.

NICK. Libby. Wouldn't it be wonderful if she was right.

LIBBY. Who?

NICK. Judy. Mum. Imagine if that bird really was a sign and our lives were going to turn around and become wonderful.

LIBBY. Nick, please don't start listening to all her bullshit.

NICK. I see signs in everything. For you and me. Mystic, wonderful, amazing things are going to happen.

LIBBY *smiles in spite of herself. A warm moment passes between them.*

LIBBY. Bring the tray.

She heads into the house, leaving NICK *alone. He looks out across the garden. Suddenly, his eye is caught by something across the garden. He stands slowly, watching in amazement as a* BOY *of about nineteen comes padding up the path. He is wearing just a swimming costume and his body is glowing wet.* NICK *stares as the boy half-nods to him in a shy greeting, drops a key under a plant pot on the terrace, and sprints off down the path. The lights snap to black.*

Scene Two

Bright sunshine. The garden is the same except for a cool box,
dumped on the grass. DR PETER ORAM *is standing on the sun*
terrace. He's wearing a shirt and underpants. He's looking
through an old pair of binoculars. LIBBY *enters carrying*
PETER*'s trousers.*

PETER. I've got an erection.

LIBBY. Another one?

PETER. I'm trying to find – Ah. Okay. The pink one is David
   Dimbleby's, right? I like what they've done with the back
   wall. Like a sort of conservatory. All glass. And that one. The
   white one. That must be the eye surgeon.

LIBBY. That was Mrs Lake.

PETER. Janet's been in there collecting for cystic fibrosis. Look
   at their boathouse. That's beautiful. He could make a little
   guest annex out of that. Now, where's the children's author?

LIBBY. We used to know all those people.

   He turns and looks at her.

PETER. This is my favourite view.

LIBBY. Go home to your wife.

PETER. My wife thinks I'm at the bedside of a dying patient.

LIBBY. Isn't that a little bit tasteless?

PETER. It's a fictional patient. Let's make love out here. It'd be
   like fucking in a double-page spread of *Country Life*.

   There's a noise from inside.

   Shit.

LIBBY. Put your fucking trousers on!

He grabs the trousers and disappears into the garden. NICK *pads in.*

NICK. I've still got this rash.

LIBBY. It's mites. How many times do I have to tell you? Use the cream.

NICK. I have the weirdest dreams in this house. What does it mean when you're constantly being chased?

LIBBY. I have no idea.

NICK. Sometimes I can see the person's face and sometimes I can't. Last night it was Elaine Paige.

He's taken a can from the cool box.

LIBBY. Is that your breakfast?

NICK. It's a *light* cider.

LIBBY. We're making real inroads into this mess today. I mean it. Music room. Hall. Kitchen.

JUDY (*off*). *Libby!*

LIBBY. What was she saying to you last night? After I went to bed.

NICK. Nothing.

LIBBY. Nothing?

NICK. The usual. Something about a monk.

LIBBY. I think she's keeping something from us.

NICK. What?

LIBBY. I'm not sure. She had a letter yesterday from Lawrence's.

NICK. Who?

LIBBY. The solicitors. She took it straight upstairs and read it. In private.

NICK. So?

LIBBY. So. It worries me. Has she ever said anything to you about her plans?

NICK *shakes his head.*

Are you sure?

NICK. Jesus, Libby, I've just got up.

LIBBY. I think she's trying to sell it.

NICK. I didn't think –

LIBBY. She can do what she likes with it. There was no new will. It doesn't matter what was *intended*.

JUDY (*off*). *Libby!*

NICK. Why would she sell it? It's ours, Libby. It's going to be ours.

LIBBY. You know that, do you, Nick? You have it in writing?

Beat. NICK *looks at her.*

Who knows what her finances are like? Who knows what's going on inside her head?

Beat. NICK*'s listening.*

She can't be trusted. Jesus, Nick, do I seriously have to remind you of all the times she's lied to us? Do I?

NICK *shakes his head. An acceptance.*

I want you to talk to her.

NICK. Me?

LIBBY. Find out what she's up to.

NICK. No. Libby –

LIBBY. Listen. This is our future, alright? The only thing we have left.

JUDY (*off*). *There's a tremendous column of ants in this kitchen.*

LIBBY. Or is that why you came here? To clean the place up so she can sell it out from under you?

NICK. No –

LIBBY. Then tell her. Make it clear that you didn't come here for that. Tell her, Nick.

NICK. Alright.

JUDY (*off*). *There must be a nest.*

LIBBY *wearily heads off into the house.*

LIBBY. You need to put the powder in the *corners*. I keep telling you.

NICK *goes to the upturned plant pot. He's about to lift it when* SUMMER *appears.*

SUMMER. Why do they have to shout?

NICK. What?

SUMMER. Did all that smack make you deaf? They shout like a pair of insane people.

NICK (*leaving*). I tune it out, Summer, darling. It's white noise.

LIBBY (*off*). *Summer?*

SUMMER. Well, you're fucking lucky.

SUMMER *goes over to the plant pot. She looks underneath, then exits.*

LIBBY (*off*). *I want you to find the bin-liners and tear them off. Everyone's pitching in today – Nick, as well.*

PETER *appears with his trousers on.*

JUDY (*off*). *Or are they weevils, do you think, Libby?*

LIBBY (*off*). *What?*

JUDY (*off*). *Weevils swarm.*

PETER *runs to the door. He quotes the first few lines from 'The Times They Are a-Changin'" by Bob Dylan.*

JUDY *appears. He raises his fist in salute.*

For God's sake.

PETER. Didn't you hear the gunshots? They've risen up and seized the Spar shop.

JUDY. At last.

PETER. All they need now is strong leadership. Get your poncho quick and something to wave.

JUDY. You're absolutely wonderful, Peter.

PETER. Hello, my darling.

They kiss and hug. She squeezes him.

JUDY. Rugby arms.

PETER. Did I leave my guitar here last week?

JUDY. Libby – ?

She turns back to PETER.

Let's fuck off somewhere and take acid.

PETER. Where would I find acid?

JUDY. You're a doctor.

PETER. I'd have to score it off one of my sons.

LIBBY *appears with bin bags of junk.*

JUDY. Did Peter leave his guitar here last week?

LIBBY. I have no idea.

JUDY. Well, let's look for it, shall we?

LIBBY. We're cleaning.

JUDY. Yes, but we haven't started yet.

PETER. Hello, Libby. Seems like ages since I last saw you.

LIBBY. We're having a system today, do you understand me? We're going to get everything out of that music room and sort it through properly. Out here on the step. A proper blitz.

JUDY. Don't use the language of the Nazis, Libby. I don't enjoy it.

PETER. When am I ever going to get over this view?

JUDY. I want you to come up here when there's a harvest moon, Peter. It bears down like it's going to collide with you. It's wonderful. Huge. Orange.

PETER. Aha. The man from Atlantis.

DANIEL, the boy from the end of Scene One appears. He has a bundle of letters in his hand.

JUDY. Daniel darling. Are you a little bit later today?

DANIEL. My mum –

JUDY. Is she alright?

PETER. Tell her I'll be in to see her soon. Okay? Tell her she needs to keep those exercises up. Moving the wrists and the ankles. Yes?

DANIEL nods again.

DANIEL. I'll –

JUDY. Yes, of course, Daniel. Go ahead.

He goes to the plant pot and scoops an old rusty key from under it, then exits across the garden.

LIBBY. That boy gives me the creeps.

JUDY. Libby, no.

LIBBY. I'm sorry. He does. Sloping up that path, day after day –

JUDY. Peter brought him here. Honestly, Libby, his mother is obese, poor thing. She has the most terrible depression. She has asthma, diabetes –

PETER. She's now totally bed-bound, I'm afraid.

JUDY. You see? Honestly. He looks after that woman –

PETER. He's nineteen.

JUDY. I think he's entitled to let off a bit of steam in our pool.

PETER. The thing is with Daniel –

JUDY. You don't need to justify yourself, Peter. He cleaned that pool himself, didn't he? And he's fitted a brand-new filter.

PETER. His mother's started making noises again –

JUDY. Oh no.

PETER. About keeping him home. And if he can't train, he can't compete.

JUDY. It's such a waste.

PETER. I'll talk to him. But what he needs, is someone up here every day. Pushing him on. Encouraging him.

JUDY. A father.

PETER. Exactly. Not that I –

JUDY. Why not, Peter? Who better than you? Who better?

LIBBY (*almost to herself*). *His own?*

PETER. I don't mind doing it. I just – I don't want to be a nuisance.

JUDY. What? You're always welcome here, Peter. Isn't he, Libby?

PETER. Am I, Libby?

JUDY. As long as your wife doesn't mind.

PETER. She's already convinced that I'm having an affair with you.

JUDY. If only you were.

LIBBY. Mother, please.

JUDY. My children hate it when I'm sexual. It frightens them.

LIBBY. It frightens everyone.

PETER. What the boy needs, of course, is to escape his
mother's clutches. Permanently. And that place – My God. I
mean, the smell alone –

JUDY (*hurriedly*). Daniel, did you forget something?

They all turn to see DANIEL *standing at the edge of the
path.* DANIEL *holds up the bundle of letters.*

Oh – the post. Yes, of course. How sweet of you to bring it up.

PETER. You ought to be an assassin, young man. That silent
approach.

He hands the bundle of letters to JUDY, *then turns back
towards the pool house.*

Fuck.

JUDY. He didn't hear you.

PETER. I think I'd better – Oh, shit – You really don't think – ?

JUDY. You caught yourself. I promise.

He goes. JUDY *turns back to* LIBBY, *the letters still in her
hand.*

Isn't he wonderful? Hull, originally. Other people wouldn't
have got involved, but he saw that boy was depressed,
actually depressed, and he thought, right – what can we – ?
Swimming medals. Okay. He came marching up that path
demanding to know about our pool. We hit it off like the
oldest of friends. I adore him.

LIBBY. What about the wife?

JUDY. What about her?

LIBBY. Is she nice?

JUDY. She sails. Got herself on all the committees. They have a
wonderful social life.

JUDY shoves the letters into her dressing-gown pocket.

LIBBY *watches*.

LIBBY. Not going to open them?

JUDY. I was saying to Nicky, we ought to go down into the town once in a while. Don't you think? The Old Jerusalem? They have a folk night now – That blind woman from Brixham. And they do Thai food.

LIBBY. Nicky's not going to be here, Mother. Not for much longer.

JUDY *stops and looks up*.

JUDY. What do you mean?

LIBBY. Exactly what I say.

JUDY. Has he said something?

LIBBY. He doesn't have to. I know Nick, Mother, and I know he has a very specific reason for being here.

JUDY. What reason?

NICK *appears with a glass of wine in his hand. Beat.* LIBBY *heads off*.

LIBBY. All those boxes in the music room are going to have to come out – we'll do it in stages.

She gives NICK *a significant look as she heads indoors.*

And we need more Cif.

NICK. God, it's hot.

JUDY (*removing her dressing gown*). Isn't it wonderful? I keep thinking of Poona. That funny little station. Need to find a nice shady spot for a Masala tea and a cigarette.

NICK *lifts the plant pot.* JUDY *looks round to see* NICK *just replacing it*.

Did you want to go swimming, darling?

NICK. What?

JUDY. The pool house is open. Daniel's in there.

NICK. No, I just – I wasn't even –

He walks over to a seat. JUDY *looks as though she's had a revelation. She dumps her dressing gown on the back of a chair.*

JUDY. Isn't Daniel a nice boy? Not a boy, really. A young man. Do you think he's – ? I wondered if you could tell. I mean, he's terribly sensitive, isn't he? Shy.

Beat.

And he lives with his mother.

NICK. I have absolutely no idea what you're talking about.

JUDY. He's been coming here an awful lot more these days.

NICK. Has he?

JUDY. Yes. Since you've moved in.

NICK. I hope you're not thinking –

JUDY. Oh, darling. I'm only –

NICK. Because you can forget it. Absolutely.

JUDY. No. You mustn't – darling – to close your heart –

NICK. I mean it. No. No.

JUDY. You have to keep it open, Nicky. Your spirit – And you have the most extraordinary spirit – you take after me in that. I'm only saying that Daniel, whatever you might think of him, has started coming up to the house more. He has. And later too – later in the mornings. I've noticed it. Perhaps – I'm not saying for definite, but – perhaps – he wants to see more of the people who live here.

NICK. It's Summer.

JUDY. He hasn't said two words to Summer. Not two words.

Little beat.

Courage, darling. That's the one thing all lovers have. Courage. The heart runs on it. And why shouldn't he come here looking for you? Why shouldn't he? When you're so beautiful.

She takes a can of cider out and opens it. Silence.

You're just like me. I had a younger lover. He stayed in my tent for almost two years. He was a wonderful photographer and a cook and he could fix up any kind of motorbike. And he made me laugh –

DANIEL *appears.* JUDY *stands, astonished and delighted, as though she'd conjured him.*

DANIEL. Sorry. The filter's blocked. If you've got, like, a – Phillips screwdriver?

NICK *stands.*

JUDY. No, darling. I'll go. It's funny, I can't always picture his face, but I can remember other things so clearly.

She stops.

He had courage. And grace. And very tight little balls like a Bullmastiff.

She goes. An uncomfortable silence.

NICK. Do you want a cider?

DANIEL *shakes his head. Silence.*

I'm surprised you don't get bored.

Silence.

I used to hate this house. When I was your age, I mean. Libby and I were always plotting our escape.

Silence.

Shoplift some eye make-up – that was the plan – and go and find David Sylvian. He's a musician. Was. Is? Libby had quite a thing for David Sylvian. Hard to imagine now.

Silence.

In the end, of course, I was the one who ended up leaving.

Although that was less to do with pop stars and more to do
with –

Little beat.

– amphetamines.

LIBBY *arrives and holds out a screwdriver.*

LIBBY. I hope that's big enough.

DANIEL *grabs it and leaves.* NICK *looks a bit shell-
shocked.*

Did you speak to her?

NICK. What?

SUMMER *appears.*

LIBBY. Did you speak to her? Did you speak to Mum about the
house?

NICK. Sorry. Just a minute –

LIBBY. Nick – ?

NICK. Sorry, I – I feel a bit sick.

He's gone. We hear JUDY *from inside.*

JUDY (*off*). *I've just discovered something very worrying,
Libby.*

SUMMER. What's the matter with him?

JUDY (*off*). *Are you there? This smell. Summer's right, it's
worse. Do you think something's died?*

LIBBY. Yes, me.

JUDY (*off*). *I'm wondering if we shouldn't get the floor up.*

JUDY *appears.*

We need a cat, Libby. Slip underneath. Or a Jack Russell,
they don't care, they'll eat anything. Better than vultures.

LIBBY (*seeing the cider can*). Are you drinking?

JUDY (*turning back inside*). We're all drinking, Libby. It's a lovely bright summer's day.

She goes back in. LIBBY *looks at the sacks.*

SUMMER. I think you ought to know, I've made a decision about my dad's.

LIBBY. Summer, that subject is not open for discussion.

SUMMER. I'm not going

JUDY (*off*). *Libby, follow me with some newspaper, will you?*

LIBBY. I don't know why I'm bothering with this.

SUMMER. There are parents who let their children make their own decisions, you know. They consider it to be healthy.

LIBBY. Summer, you are going to your father's.

SUMMER. Why are you such a bitch to me?

LIBBY. I beg your pardon?

SUMMER. Do you think I'm stupid? Jesus Christ – I know why you want me out of the way –

LIBBY. I don't want you out of the way –

SUMMER. Just do yourself a favour, yeah? Try not to make so much of a fool of yourself this time.

LIBBY. *What?*

SUMMER. With that doctor.

LIBBY *sits. There's an exhausted little silence.*

LIBBY. Summer –

SUMMER. Have some self-respect.

LIBBY. Summer, come and sit down.

SUMMER *doesn't move.*

When Judy was at college she had a lecturer. An economist. He was older than her. Sit down, please.

SUMMER *comes and sits on the step.*

She was his pupil. And he seduced her. She never finished her degree, she ran off and lived with him in a little flat in London. Something nobody did back then. Not women, anyway. And that's what got her into radical politics. They made a newspaper together. A political newspaper. They sold it on the street.

SUMMER. What newspaper?

LIBBY. Nothing. They – Nobody bought it.

Beat.

And they had two children together. And when the youngest was only two weeks old, he left her. And he married someone else. And that was my father. And I never knew him.

SUMMER. I know.

Silence.

LIBBY. I want you to see your father because it's important. Because he's asked to see you and that's – important.

SUMMER. But why now?

LIBBY. Who knows?

SUMMER. He's never wanted to see me up till now.

LIBBY. Well, as people get older they start to look at life a little differently.

SUMMER. After fifteen years?

LIBBY. Well, yes. And I believe he has a new relationship. A wife.

SUMMER. What's that got to do with it?

LIBBY. Well, she obviously – It's often the women who bring about – Who knows? Maybe she wants to start a family herself. Maybe she wants to see what kind of father he is.

SUMMER. I could tell her.

LIBBY. So could I.

SUMMER. We're alright on our own, though, aren't we? We don't need anyone else.

LIBBY. Of course. I just – This is something I think you ought to do.

Little beat.

SUMMER. You'll miss me.

LIBBY. Of course I will.

SUMMER. And keep your hands off that doctor.

LIBBY. I'm not going near him.

SUMMER. Promise?

LIBBY. I promise.

LIBBY *pulls* SUMMER *in close and kisses the top of her head.* DANIEL *appears at the bottom of the garden. As soon as she sees him,* SUMMER *gets up from her position.* LIBBY *gets up too.*

Coming in?

SUMMER *shakes her head.*

Don't be too long.

LIBBY *exits.* DANIEL *starts to walk past.*

SUMMER. You look after your mum, don't you?

He stops.

So do I.

DANIEL. My mum can't move.

SUMMER. I can actually see that having certain advantages.

Silence. DANIEL *is about to turn away when* SUMMER *speaks again.*

Why don't you ever come up in the evenings? It's more of a laugh then.

He turns. Silence.

You have to catch them at the right time, but – between six and eight. That's the window. When they're pissed, but –

A noise from inside, voices.

– not too pissed.

JUDY (*off*). Nicky. Nicky.

LIBBY *appears. Anxious.*

LIBBY. Summer, have you seen your uncle?

SUMMER. No.

LIBBY. Are you sure?

SUMMER. What's happened?

JUDY *appears. She's extremely distressed.*

JUDY. All his clothes are still there.

LIBBY (*shouting across the garden*). Nicky?

JUDY. But there's some gin gone.

LIBBY. What?

JUDY. Two bottles of gin. They were in the pantry, but they've gone.

SUMMER. What's going on?

JUDY. What have you done, Libby?

LIBBY. Me?

JUDY. What have you done? You've driven him away.

LIBBY. *What?*

JUDY. With your constant talk of the house – your suspicions. Nicky isn't like you, Libby. He's not materialistic.

LIBBY. This is hilarious.

JUDY. He couldn't stand it any longer.

SUMMER. Shouldn't somebody go and look for him?

LIBBY. Do you want to know what Nick couldn't stand? Your lies.

JUDY. Don't you dare –

SUMMER *heads off down the path.*

LIBBY. Your lies. You have no right to this house – How dare you? It's ours. Mine. Mine and Nicky's.

LIBBY *marches over to the post, snatches it up. Starts tearing it open.*

JUDY. What's – ? Are you – ?

LIBBY. Foxtons. Singer's. Look – Do you think I'm stupid?

JUDY. How dare you –

LIBBY. These are all from estate agents.

JUDY. How dare you look at my correspondence?

She storms over to snatch the letters. LIBBY *clings onto them. An ugly tussle.* JUDY *wrenches them away from* LIBBY.

LIBBY. You cannot possibly try to hold the moral / high-ground here –

JUDY. My private correspondence? Addressed to me?

LIBBY. Yes – you. Your secret little deals.

JUDY. What right have you – ?

LIBBY. This house is ours. You can't sell this house. Okay? It's ours. It's ours.

PETER *appears.*

PETER. What the hell's going on?

LIBBY. Peter, this is none of your business.

JUDY. No. I want you to stay, Peter – I want you to hear a mother being accused –

LIBBY. Why don't you open the letters?

Little beat.

JUDY. I beg your pardon?

LIBBY. If you're so outraged –

We hear SUMMER *calling down the path.*

SUMMER (*off*). *Nick? Nick!*

JUDY. Alright. Yes. If it makes you happy –

(*Pulling letters out.*) 'An exciting opportunity – ' This is
from Singer's – 'to invest in a range of executive one- and
two-bedroom new-build apartments with outstanding estuary
views.' It's a circular.

She hands the letter to PETER *for verification. He nods.*

PETER. We get a lot of these –

LIBBY. What about the other one?

JUDY. 'Longer opening hours. We're opening our branches at
times to suit you. Easier viewings. More convenient
appointments.' – Good for you, Foxtons.

Little silence.

LIBBY. Let me tell you something. If I ever do find out –

JUDY. Don't threaten me –

LIBBY. – That you are trying to sell this house – I'm *warning*
you. I will fight you.

JUDY. Oh, for God's sake, Libby –

LIBBY. I will fight you.

JUDY *walks over to* LIBBY.

JUDY. I have often thought – And I don't want you to take this
in the wrong way – that some kind of spiritual dimension –
might – perhaps – Bring a little bit of peace into your life.

Little silence.

PETER. Well. I often think that to air these arguments – these –
inevitable tensions – I mean, you should hear my lads –

JUDY. Peter, would you like a glass of wine?

PETER. Erm –

JUDY. Come into the house. We'll have a little rest, shall we? After all that screaming.

She sets off. LIBBY *calls after her.*

LIBBY. Grandpa was going to change his will, you know. Cut you out completely. But by the time the solicitor came up here, he was already unconscious.

The two women stare at each other.

PETER. Libby – listen – I know this is none of my business –

LIBBY. It's not, Peter. You're right. Why don't you go home?

He nods. Starts to exit. SUMMER*'s voice again.*

SUMMER (*off*). *Nick! Nick!*

PETER *turns to* JUDY.

PETER. I'll see if I can –

JUDY. Oh yes, Peter. Would you?

LIBBY. They'll never find him. He knows those little paths. Grandpa could never find him. No one will. He's gone.

JUDY (*murderous*). Jesus Christ, Libby, if I knew what you'd said to him –

LIBBY. He saw you, Mother. He didn't need me to say a word. He saw – To get your children here as unpaid labour, then to sell the house from under them – their birthright. Why the hell should he stay? He's right. Fair fucking play to him. That's the first bit of backbone he's ever shown.

SUMMER*'s cries again; more urgent, louder now.*

SUMMER (*off*). *Nick!*

JUDY. I just wish that you could find a little bit of softness in your heart, Libby. Somewhere. Because it's that hardness, that coldness which makes it so difficult – I think – for you to ever hold on to anyone.

Beat. JUDY *walks into the house.* SUMMER*'s cries, desperate in the distance.*

SUMMER (*off*). *Nick! Nick!*

LIBBY *sets off down the path when an overwhelming convulsion of rage takes her. She stops and converts it into a call for* NICK. *A scream.*

LIBBY (*screamed*). NICKY!

Lights snap to black.

Scene Three

Night. A little party is in full swing. JUDY, LIBBY *and* PETER *are dressed in clothes that have been liberated from the bin-liners; vintage stuff, hunting pink, tuxedos, etc.* PETER *has a carousel of slides in his arms. Beside him, on the floor, is a slide projector. He's drunk and exhilarated.*

PETER. I was nineteen years old. I was dressed not dissimilarly to the way I am now, only I had a flat stomach and hair down to here. And I was walking over the brow of this little hill. I'd lost my friends. Which, without wishing to sound cruel, was – well. They were the College's cerebral set, if you know what I mean. They played 'Risk'. Competitively. They wore polar necks and had pimply beards.

JUDY. Poor things.

PETER. And I was flying. Fuck. Do you remember Afghani Black – ?

JUDY. Yes! All sticky and packed into a pipe.

LIBBY. Anyway.

PETER. Anyway. I – Yes. Where was I?

LIBBY. A hill.

PETER. I came over this hill and, before me, all spread out – I
  remember thinking to myself, this must be what a battle
  looks like, you know? This mass of people, this – incredible.
  It looked – Napoleonic. And there was music. Thudding.
  And the sunshine. I don't remember who was playing. We
  were too early for Dylan and we'd missed Hendrix. It had
  taken us two fucking days to get there. And then this girl
  with red hair just floated into my path and said –

Beat.

  – who fucking knows what she said but she took my hand
  and – she had these friends, this group, and they were talking
  about the world in this way – I'd never heard people talk like
  that. With such a – Jesus, the *imagination* of it. The sense of
  possibility. They –

JUDY. I know.

PETER. Of course you do. And we danced. And she took off
  her T-shirt, and she had these beautiful breasts. Oh my God.
  And I thought – Why not? Why shouldn't the world just
  change? Why shouldn't we change it?

LIBBY. You and the girl?

PETER. What exactly is stopping us – Yes, me and the girl –
  from uprooting the whole fucking system?

JUDY. Hosanna!

PETER. And I thought of my dad. Weirdly. With these perfect
  little tits jigging around in front of me. I thought – That
  world. His bicycle clips. And the *Daily Express*. And my
  smiling, suffering mum. I thought – An image flashed into
  my head. Of my mum. Choosing lino. She'd picked out *new*
  lino for the *new* kitchen in their *new* house and it was – I
  don't know. I'm drunk.

He fiddles with the carousel.

JUDY. Go on.

PETER. Little flowers. Cramped inside a little square. You know? Little, conforming flowers. Oppressed. And I thought, yeah. That fucking just about sums it up.

JUDY. Little flowers.

PETER. Bring it on! I thought. Bring on the revolution. Let's – Even my mum. Why not? A new world order. Peace. Justice. For all. That's what I thought. Felt.

LIBBY. And did you?

PETER. What?

LIBBY. Bring about a new world order?

JUDY. Libby –

PETER. No. I'm afraid I – Ha! I joined the Labour Party.

JUDY. You saved people's lives.

PETER. I didn't really do anything.

LIBBY. But what about now?

PETER. Erm –

LIBBY. Do you still have hope?

JUDY. Don't interrogate, Libby.

LIBBY. You're asking questions.

JUDY. Yes, but it's a tone you have.

PETER. I really don't know. I – Hope. Have you?

JUDY. Of course!

PETER. Yes! Well – that's why you're the true revolutionary, my darling. Me? I look at my sons and I think – these boys, you know, they've had the finest – every fucking opportunity lavished on them. And what are they interested in? What are they passionate about? Fuck all. Nazis and sharks.

He takes the carousel off the projector.

This is not going to work.

LIBBY. I'll find you another one.

JUDY. And bring out some crackers, Libby, and something to spread on them.

LIBBY. Some people spend their birthdays being waited on.

She's gone.

JUDY. You're a tonic, Peter. I'm mad about you. Totally crazy.

PETER. I talked to her. I'm afraid I think you're right.

Little silence.

JUDY. She's going?

PETER. She sees no reason to stay. Nick's gone. Summer's gone –

JUDY. Well, let her go. If she thinks she can hold me to ransom. No. No, I'm not afraid of being on my own.

PETER. Do you mind if I give you a bit of advice? You can tell me to piss off if you like.

JUDY. I wouldn't dream of it.

PETER. Give it to her.

Silence.

This house. The one thing she wants. Give it to her. Tell her she can have it. Now. Tonight. On her birthday.

JUDY. She wouldn't believe me if I did.

PETER. She would.

JUDY. She thinks I'm a liar. She doesn't trust me. She thinks I'd tell her anything.

PETER. Then give it to her. Actually – There are ways. Believe me. I know people who could draw up a document. Make it hers. Legally.

JUDY. And what about me?

PETER. You could be secured. She wouldn't – Listen. You can be secured. Here. Until the day of your death.

JUDY. And this would make her happy?

PETER. Yes.

JUDY. And what about Nicky? He'll come home, Peter. I know him. I know my child. Eventually –

PETER. Nicky is a wonderful person.

JUDY. He's a romantic.

PETER. But if you're looking for someone to be responsible. To take on the burden of this house –

JUDY nods gently.

JUDY. Do you think I'm stubborn?

PETER. No.

JUDY. Or ridiculous?

PETER. And you. You would be lighter. Freer.

JUDY. Do you think of me as old? As an old bag?

PETER. I want to help you. Please. Let me arrange it. It could be my gift.

JUDY. You want her to stay here, don't you? You don't want her to run away again.

PETER. I want to tell you something. This house. This summer. I feel as though I've been in a coma for the last God knows how many years. Honestly. And I'm now finally waking up.

Beat.

I want *you* to be happy.

Beat.

And her too. Yes. You, wise woman. I want that.

LIBBY *appears with another carousel.* JUDY *and* PETER *break.*

LIBBY. There *is* a rat.

JUDY. No.

LIBBY. Or a fox. You stand in that kitchen and you can hear it. Just outside the door.

JUDY. For God's sake.

LIBBY. I'm telling you. We'll start spreading the black death next, and you can be the one who explains it to the council.

She hands PETER *the carousel.*

'Mixed family', this one says. Something of an understatement.

JUDY. Turn off the light, Libby.

LIBBY. What?

JUDY. In the solarium. Quick. It has to be dark.

LIBBY *goes and turns the light off in the solarium.* PETER *attaches the wheel and a huge picture appears on the wall. It's a black-and-white 1930s picture of three women.*

Aha! Now then.

LIBBY. Is that Granny?

JUDY. My mother, Peter. The villain of the piece.

LIBBY. Don't be ridiculous.

JUDY. She was a monster, Libby.

LIBBY. Rubbish. She didn't suffer fools, that's all.

JUDY. Or Jews. Or homosexuals. Or any kind of foreigner. Apart from that, she was a kitten.

Click. A King Charles spaniel.

PETER. Aah!

LIBBY. Kimbo!

JUDY. Hello, Kim.

LIBBY. She was a marvellous dog.

Click. Another shot of Kim.

Look. Isn't she beautiful?

Click. Kim again. Then – Mr and Mrs Haussman with friends at the captain's table, 1930s.

JUDY. Now. She was my mother's bridesmaid – I remember this.

LIBBY. Look at the diamonds.

JUDY. She sang. And she was related to Harold Macmillan. And something terrible happened to her in Canada.

Click. A very sulky seven-year-old girl. Arms crossed. Absolute defiance on her face.

Oh my God!

PETER. Is that you?

LIBBY. Judith Haussman aged seven.

JUDY. Look how furious I was. I hated having my picture taken.

PETER. Strong spirit.

JUDY. I loathed it. I was ready to kill.

Click. JUDY, a few years later. She is smiling now.

LIBBY. That's a bit more like it.

JUDY. I was nine then. My father took that with a funny little Kodak out there on the lawn. I remember it like yesterday.

PETER. You've cheered up a bit.

JUDY. I'd started masturbating.

Click. Kim on a rug. Click. Kim in a car.

Jesus, that sodding dog.

Click. A black-and-white photograph of a large store at the turn of the century.

Haussman's!

LIBBY. Oh my God –

JUDY. 1906. That's Meers Road. Bristol.

LIBBY. Oh, to be back there.

JUDY. No thank you. I don't want their blood money.

LIBBY. Don't be ridiculous, Mother. They sold curtain rods.

PETER. I wonder what that shop is now.

JUDY. I hope it's the headquarters of some revolutionary terrorist cell. I hope the people of Bristol have risen up and seized it.

LIBBY. It's a Pizza Express.

A swift click. JUDY *in school uniform.*

PETER. Head girl.

JUDY. I was anything but, Peter.

LIBBY. She gave her father a stroke.

JUDY. Don't be sensational, Libby.

LIBBY. He was constantly worried about her and then he keeled over. It was the stress.

JUDY. Malt whisky and cigars gave him a stroke.

LIBBY. He was totally paralysed. He had to have his bottom wiped. Which, for a proud man, is intolerable.

JUDY. I shouldn't think it's a walk in the park for anyone.

Click. LIBBY *and* NICK *as children.*

LIBBY. Oh my God, I remember that Christmas –

PETER. Is that you?

JUDY. Look at Nicky. Look at my beautiful boy.

LIBBY. See how fat I was?

JUDY. Libby was a terrible snacker, Peter –

PETER. I'm amazed.

JUDY. The nuns had to hide anything sweet.

LIBBY. How would you know?

JUDY. Icing sugar, marzipan – toothpaste.

LIBBY. That's total rubbish.

There's the sound of a crash or a thud from inside the house.

Jesus Christ –

JUDY. What was that?

PETER (*setting off*). It was outside, wasn't it?

LIBBY. Just be careful.

JUDY. Yes, be careful, Peter. Please.

He goes. They listen.

LIBBY. It's the rat.

JUDY. Don't be so silly.

LIBBY. I'm telling you. They get blasé if they're not exterminated. They get bolder and bolder until they take over the whole house.

JUDY. In Bangladesh, maybe.

LIBBY. This house is *like* Bangladesh. I keep telling you.

JUDY. Sssh –

LIBBY. When the council come back here –

JUDY. Be quiet –

She listens. The sound of voices off.

LIBBY. Oh my God.

JUDY. Who is it?

LIBBY. It's kids.

She looks at JUDY.

It's kids – They've broken in.

JUDY (*getting up*). Rubbish.

LIBBY. They saw that the lights were off and they've broken in. That's what they do. Gangs.

JUDY *is standing now, both are nervous.* PETER *appears.*

PETER. Little surprise for you both.

NICK *comes on after him, rather sheepishly.*

LIBBY. Nick!

JUDY. Nicky!

JUDY *rushes up to him. He looks far worse than he ever has. He has a black eye and very dirty clothes and is trembling slightly.*

LIBBY. Oh my God. Where have you been?

JUDY. Look at you – Oh, my darling – You're wet.

LIBBY. Jesus, Nicky –

JUDY. You're wet through.

NICK. It's just a little accident. Try not to – Happy birthday, darling.

JUDY. Oh, isn't that wonderful? For your birthday, Libby –

LIBBY. Yes –

JUDY. What a wonderful, thoughtful surprise.

NICK. I'm sorry.

JUDY. What?

NICK. I shouldn't have just fucked off.

JUDY. It doesn't matter about that now.

NICK. I should have behaved in a more gentlemanly fashion.

JUDY. It doesn't matter, darling. You're home now. That's all we care about.

NICK. What's this?

JUDY. A slide show.

NICK. Good for you. We must take our pleasures where we can –

He suddenly dry retches.

JUDY. Nicky –

NICK. It's fine. I'm just a little – It's my stomach.

LIBBY. Have you eaten anything?

NICK. Gaviscon. I chew the little tablets – they're very sustaining.

LIBBY. I'm going to get you something –

NICK. No, thank you, Libby. Mother, darling, could I have a little drink, please?

JUDY. Peter's brought some rather nice champagne –

NICK. I'd prefer to have gin. Libby, are you having a nice day?

LIBBY. Yes, thank you.

NICK. I really should have brought you something. Isn't Summer here?

LIBBY. She's in France.

NICK. What?

JUDY. She went to her father's, darling, remember? We never hear from her, do we, Libby? So we assume she's having the most marvellous time.

LIBBY. Nicky, where have you been?

NICK. Plymouth.

JUDY. *Plymouth?*

LIBBY. What for?

NICK. It was a sort of dare to myself.

LIBBY. We were calling Bristol – weren't we? London –

JUDY. Did you have fun?

NICK. I don't think anyone, Mother, in the whole rambling course of human history, has ever had fun in Plymouth. Except the Luftwaffe.

LIBBY. So why did you go?

NICK. I danced a little bit close to the flame, Libby. I scared myself away. It doesn't matter, does it?

JUDY (*emotionally, embracing him*). Oh, Nicky –

NICK. Don't spill my drink.

JUDY. Do you know who I thank for this?

NICK. Some Indian god.

JUDY. Peter.

PETER. What?

JUDY. It was you, Peter. You who showed me – earlier tonight – the transforming gift of generosity. Nothing happens by accident, does it? Libby, give me your lipstick.

LIBBY. What?

JUDY. I want to bring Peter into the commune.

LIBBY. Don't be ridiculous.

NICK. Here –

   NICK *produces a lipstick from his pocket.*

JUDY. A new name.

PETER. What's going on?

JUDY. I'm giving you a name. A spiritual name. A new name which you will henceforth be known by –

   She rubs lipstick into a red spot on his forehead.

PETER. I'm honoured.

JUDY. Arjuna.

PETER. Arjuna.

JUDY. It means 'the seer'. What were your names, my darlings? They were wonderful. Bhagwan gave everyone a new name, Peter.

LIBBY. I don't remember.

JUDY. Yes, you do, Libby. You must do.

NICK. I was Ashoka.

JUDY. Yes! Ashoka!

NICK. It means 'the strong warrior'. Wasn't that insightful of him?

JUDY. I'm going to make up your bed, Nicky –

LIBBY. I'll do it.

JUDY. No –

PETER. I think I'd better leave you to it –

JUDY (*grabbing* PETER). No. Peter, I want you to stay – we have to talk. We have something very important to talk about. Oh my God – this is a day! This is a wonderful day!

LIBBY *has grabbed* NICK *and dragged him outside.*

LIBBY. You look absolutely terrible. And you stink.

She hugs him very tightly. They stand together hugging silently for a bit.

NICK. He's got his feet under the table.

LIBBY (*breaking away*). What are you talking about?

NICK. Just be careful with him. He's not quite what he makes out.

LIBBY. I don't know what you mean.

NICK. Navy blue, that one. A deep conservative streak. Take it from me, Libby, darling. A couple of weeks on the gear can give me second sight.

LIBBY. Stop talking bollocks.

Little silence.

What happened, Nick?

NICK. That boy.

LIBBY. *Daniel?*

NICK. It's all very well her going on about love and beauty – she doesn't know what it's like. For me. I'd rather die than go through all that again.

LIBBY. He's still here.

NICK. I'm alright now. I've immunised myself. I've stamped out the hope.

LIBBY. You're lucky, you know. If you'd come back a week later –

NICK. You're not going?

LIBBY. She has no intention of leaving us this house. She says she's got another spot on her leg – it's all bullshit. She's a liar. I can't put up with it any more.

Beat. NICK suddenly becomes overwhelmed.

NICK. If you go – Will you take me – ?

LIBBY. If I know where you are.

NICK. I'm here now. I'm here.

LIBBY. Then yes. I will.

Loud music suddenly blares out. Seventies rock.

Oh, for God's sake.

JUDY appears with PETER behind.

JUDY. Sannyasin disco!

LIBBY. It's too loud!

LIBBY crosses and goes into the house.

JUDY. He's home! My baby's home! Let's wake 'em up! The old rebels, eh? Let's show this younger generation what it's all about! Shall we get naked?

PETER. Absolutely!

JUDY. Want to see a bit of revolutionary pussy, darlings? Come on! We have no fears here! We are in love! We are in love with life!

She lifts her nightdress up above her head.

Get a load of that, David Dimbleby!

The music very abruptly stops.

Oh, for God's sake.

LIBBY *appears*.

LIBBY. This is no time of the night for Slade.

JUDY. Peter, I appeal to you – We're being censored. Oppressed.

LIBBY. Take Nicky up to bed.

JUDY. Peter, why don't you come upstairs and make love to me?

NICK. Come on, Mother, for God's sake –

JUDY. I feel wonderful and sad. It's the gin. I'd like to be very forcefully screwed.

LIBBY. Go to bed.

Taking NICK's *hand and heading off.*

JUDY. Nicky's home. He's home. My darling's home.

LIBBY. Do you think I ought to help them?

PETER. No.

LIBBY. But it's the blind leading the blind.

PETER *produces an envelope, hands it to* LIBBY.

What's this?

PETER. Happy birthday.

LIBBY. Do you know, in all the excitement, I'd almost
forgotten –

She open the card. Reads.

That's obscene.

PETER. It's erotic.

LIBBY. In order for something to be erotic –

He kisses her very passionately.

PETER. You asked me earlier if I had hope –

LIBBY. Did I?

PETER. Well, I do. I do now. I believe that incredible things are
going to happen.

More kissing. They graduate to the floor, PETER *on top.*
LIBBY *suddenly stops.*

What's the matter?

LIBBY. Sssh.

PETER. What?

LIBBY. Listen –

LIBBY *listens. Silence.*

Get off.

PETER. What?

LIBBY. Get off!

He does. They both listen.

PETER. There's nothing there.

LIBBY. Shut up.

PETER. It's your phantom rat again.

LIBBY. Hello?

DANIEL emerges out of the shadows of the garden. LIBBY stuffs the card into her pocket.

Daniel?

DANIEL. Sorry. I was – I just – I came up to drop this –

LIBBY. Oh.

DANIEL. It's for you. It's for your birthday.

LIBBY. Goodness. Well. That really is – There really wasn't any need –

He walks forward and offers a bag.

Would you, erm – would you like a drink, or something?

DANIEL. Erm –

PETER. He won't drink, will he? The athlete. Never touches it.

LIBBY. Champagne, perhaps? Or gin – ?

PETER. You're wasting your time. I've been trying to get him to have a pint with me for months, haven't I, lad? That body's a temple.

DANIEL. I've been drinking beer.

PETER. Have you?

DANIEL. In The Old Jerusalem.

PETER. That's a great little boozer.

DANIEL. It's a shithole. It's full of Poles and Albanians.

There's a slightly uncomfortable pause.

Are you going to open your present?

LIBBY puts her hand inside the bag. She pulls out a CD.

LIBBY. Ha!

PETER. What is it?

LIBBY (*examining it with quiet amazement*). David Sylvian.

PETER. Do you like him?

LIBBY. I did. 'Red Guitar.' I did, I loved him.

She looks at DANIEL, *her face alight with the*
unexpectedness.

What an incredible thing.

PETER. It's very thoughtful.

LIBBY. Certainly more thoughtful than some of the things I've
received this evening. What on earth made you think of it?

DANIEL. I just –

LIBBY. Do you like him yourself? Well, I'm thrilled. I really
am. Completely thrilled.

She kisses him on the cheek. Beat.

PETER. Your mum's alright, is she, Daniel?

DANIEL. What?

PETER. On her own. This late.

DANIEL. She doesn't – Yeah. She usually – She doesn't wake
up – not – till –

He looks at his watch. An anguished beat.

No, it's – I probably better –

PETER. Come on. I'm sure you're alright.

DANIEL. I'd better go. Honestly.

PETER. Live a little. It's okay. I only asked because –

DANIEL. No, I – I have to go. Thanks. Erm –

He heads off.

LIBBY. Thank you, Daniel.

PETER. Yes, well done.

LIBBY. Thank you – Thank you very, very much.

But he's disappeared.

That was cruel.

PETER. He's a little spy. Who knows what he was getting up to out there.

LIBBY. David Sylvian. Well. What a remarkable thing.

PETER. I'm in love with you.

She turns to him.

I don't see any point in not saying it.

He walks over and kisses her.

I do. I love you.

They kiss again. PETER *scoops* LIBBY *up. She shrieks slightly, giggles.* PETER *begins to carry her off.*

(*As they disappear.*) Arjuna.

LIBBY. Oh, for God's sake –

PETER. Dr Arjuna. The seer. My new and beautiful name.

They kiss again. PETER *carries her off. We hear their muffled, giggly conversation for a moment. Then from the dark shadows of the garden –* DANIEL *returns.*

He goes over to LIBBY's *folded-up birthday card from* PETER. *He opens and reads it. He's about to replace the card but seems to change his mind. He then takes the card, folds it up, and puts it in his own pocket. Beat. The lights snap to black.*

End of Act One.

ACT TWO

Autumn

Scene Four

Bright September morning. There is a drinks table set up in the garden. JUDY is lying on her daybed wrapped in blankets and shawls and wearing large sunglasses. She is considerably weaker than when we last saw her. NICKY is kneeling at her feet, painting her toenails. At first, there's just silence. Birdsong. Then, when JUDY speaks, it's strange. Disconnected.

JUDY. The only thing to be in life is a rebel.

NICK. Or an air hostess.

Little beat.

When I was about eleven or so – before my voice had broken, anyway – I had a recurring fantasy. Shall I tell you? I imagined slipping away from this house in one of Granny's Chanel suits, and becoming, I blush to say it, a new and mysterious weather girl on the local news. I saw it all. Even my own downfall. Late one afternoon, during a particularly heartfelt gale-force warning, my voice would suddenly break. 'Attention all shipping – ' And with my true identity revealed, the entire West Country region would swarm on the Plymouth studios – brandishing weapons, guns, flaming torches.

Beat.

I try to reason with them. Addressing them in my wobbly contralto. But – I have deceived them. It is more than they can bear. I have, after all, opened fêtes, hospices; embraced sick children. I have tap-danced on *Children in Need*. No – They tear me to pieces on Plymouth Hoe. Nothing remains of me. I am extinguished.

After a second, LIBBY *appears from the house. She looks worried.*

LIBBY. Any change?

   NICK *shakes his head.*

   That's it. I'm going to ring him.

   LIBBY *goes back into the house.*

NICK. This ought to be interesting.

JUDY. All the rebels –

NICK. Yes?

JUDY. It's – in the heart – An energy – Isn't it? Restless. Pushing forward –

NICK. You'd have liked punk. Talk about restless energy. Or rave. Some of the happiest days of my life happened then. With that crowd. It was wonderful. I tore tickets at the Whirl-Y-Gig for a while. I wore a blue-plastic wetsuit with big boots and a very dramatic smoky eye. Wonderful people. Angry. Creative. That's what I should have gone into, really. Nightclubs. If only I could have focused my energies.

Little beat.

My friend. Freda – she was a performance artist. She used to walk out on stage in a ball gown made of dustbin liners and shred her clothes into – tiny – little – strips – flay herself, if you will – to a backing track of howling dogs. Until, at last she revealed – Ta-daa! A prodigiously pierced vagina. It was a wonderful act. You would have loved her.

Beat.

'The Duchess of Cunt.'

He admires the work so far.

You're going to like this colour.

JUDY. Red – ?

NICK. Not just red. Blood red. The red of battlefields. Khmer Rouge.

DANIEL *appears with a bundle of old fairy lights. He looks happier – more at ease.*

You've made a wonderful job of that, Daniel.

DANIEL. Thank you.

NICK. You ought to go in for it. Perhaps we could have a little business. What do you think? Set design.

DANIEL. I thought we were going to start a rock band.

NICK. We were. But now that I've seen your flair for illumination. Besides – is the public really ready for me? You, of course, would be fallen upon like crusts for the starving, but me? I think I'm just a little on the challenging side. Then again, Grace Jones was an acquired taste.

DANIEL *switches the lights on from the solarium.*

Diwali!

And off again.

So brief.

DANIEL *re-emerges from the solarium.*

DANIEL. How's Judy?

NICK. She's alright. Just a bit stoned, aren't you, pet?

JUDY. Who?

NICK. Daniel.

DANIEL. You'll be alright, Jude. Don't worry.

NICK. She's lucky. Aren't you, darling?

JUDY. Me?

NICK. This is the work of only three little pills. I used to have to inject myself in the groin to get that fucked.

LIBBY *appears from the house.*

LIBBY. Oh, that's terrific, Daniel. Thanks.

DANIEL. I'll just – I'll fetch the other chairs.

He sets off across the garden.

LIBBY. He's coming.

NICK. Okay.

LIBBY. I didn't know what else to do. Dr Merkel's in the Lake District *again*, and the district nurse can't come out because it's a prescription –

NICK. It'll be fine.

LIBBY. I saw her. Did I tell you?

NICK. Who?

LIBBY. Janet Oram. We passed each other in the Co-op. She gave me a look of – Well, I've only myself to blame, I suppose – Pity. Or sadness – God knows what he said to her.

NICK. It won't be the same as last time.

LIBBY. He thinks I told her. He thinks I sent her a note to try and wreck his marriage.

Silence.

Couldn't you be here?

NICK. What?

LIBBY. Please, Nicky – I'm begging you –

NICK (*panicking*). Oh. No. Sorry, I – He'll be completely professional. I promise. He won't even mention it. And Jesus, Lib. You had a little bit of a fling, so what? His wife found out. Not an ideal scenario, but – it's not exactly the end of the world, is it? People survive these things.

Little beat.

And you're amazing at that, aren't you? You'll glide across the surface like – the great patrician – what was her name? That movie star? It'll be a triumph –

Beat.

I wish I was stronger – For you, I mean. But – Katharine Hepburn. That's the one. Be like her. Or Granny. Be a Haussman.

He goes. DANIEL *appears, carrying chairs, which he puts down around the table.*

DANIEL. I think she'll really like this.

LIBBY *turns.*

Summer. I think she'll – It's a nice idea. For a homecoming. I think she'll love it –

LIBBY *nods. She's moved by his attempt at kindness. The tears are unstoppable now.*

LIBBY. I'm just going to – erm – I think we need –

She rushes off. JUDY *stirs again.*

JUDY. The hardest thing – is to love someone who doesn't know it –

DANIEL. Judy?

JUDY. The love that you feel just burns and burns away –

DANIEL. Are you awake? Are you talking to me?

JUDY. And the love of a younger man for an older woman?

DANIEL *squats down beside her.*

It's the mind which stops you – holds you back. So – rebel against the mind. Revolt! Let the body just – take over. The heart, the flesh – the human part of you – give that the reins – The mind is king, perhaps, but the body – the body is a republic! You know that better than anyone. You – Your body – I don't know why you bother to wear clothes. You're so beautiful naked – You always – The little hairs on your legs turn gold in the sun, don't they? And when you get into bed – Your skin – your back – Of all my lovers, you were – I call you 'spectacular', yes – I offer you the great revolutionary medal –

Pause. She suddenly becomes unsettled.

What will it be like?

DANIEL. What?

JUDY *looks at* DANIEL *suddenly, as though he were a stranger.*

JUDY. What time is it? I'm –

DANIEL. It's alright, Judy –

JUDY. I feel strange –

DANIEL. Someone's coming –

JUDY. Sebastian?

DANIEL. They're just – Libby? – They're coming in a minute.

JUDY. I don't – I – I don't like it –

DANIEL. Sssh –

JUDY. Where is it? She – It ought to be –

LIBBY *comes out.*

LIBBY. Is she alright?

DANIEL. She just woke up. She got a bit upset.

LIBBY. It's alright, Mum. Peter's coming.

JUDY. What?

LIBBY. I've rung Peter. He's on his way.

JUDY. I don't understand it.

LIBBY. It's your pills.

JUDY. What?

LIBBY. You're flying. It's the dose. We have to get Peter to level out your dose.

JUDY. What?

LIBBY. It's the morphine.

Beat. JUDY *seems to understand.*

JUDY. Yes… I see.

LIBBY. Are you sure you wouldn't be more comfortable inside?

JUDY. No.

LIBBY. Where it's warm?

JUDY. No. I can't breathe in there. If I'm going to die today, I want to be able to look at this sky.

LIBBY. You're not going to die today.

JUDY. I am, Libby, I feel that I am.

LIBBY. You felt that on Friday, Mum. And on Sunday. And again yesterday afternoon when you were watching the snooker.

She walks across the garden and looks at the assembled table. DANIEL *follows her.*

DANIEL. Are you sure you don't want me to – I can take it all down.

LIBBY. No, Daniel –

DANIEL. Won't take me five minutes…

LIBBY. This is as much for you as it is for Summer. It's – This is a joint celebration. Your swimming and her coming home – No. You deserve a party –

She glances over at JUDY.

She'll be fine. She just needs –

DANIEL. She thought I was someone else. Sebastian.

LIBBY. He was – Well – He was a very important part of her life.

DANIEL. Do you think we should try and find him? I mean, if she wants to talk to him –

LIBBY. He died. A long time ago.

Little silence.

Christ, Peter's taking his time.

DANIEL. Do you want – ? If you like, I can be here with her –
When he comes –

LIBBY. No…

DANIEL. You don't have to be here.

LIBBY. That's… You're very gallant, Daniel. But I really have
to –

Silence.

Thank you.

JUDY. There's only one enemy, and there's only ever been one
– Fascism – in all its guises.

DANIEL. I wish I could – I mean, I know I'm only a –

Beat.

If I was able to –

PETER. Good morning.

PETER*'s at the bottom of the garden, carrying a medical
bag.* DANIEL *steps back again, instinctively.*

You still here, young man?

LIBBY. Daniel's been a godsend. All summer. I don't know
what we'd have done without him.

PETER. Still swimming?

DANIEL *nods.*

How's the team?

DANIEL. It's good.

PETER. Just good?

DANIEL. Yes.

PETER. Are you winning?

DANIEL. Mostly.

LIBBY. They've had a terrific season, haven't you?

PETER. Have you heard from Summer?

LIBBY. She's back today.

PETER. Oh – Well – that'll be –

Tense little silence.

LIBBY. Mum, Peter's here –

PETER. Hello, Judy –

LIBBY. Daniel, would you mind, just – See if you can find something for those chairs, erm – Some cushions or something. Something clean.

He sets off into the house.

PETER (*to* JUDY). How are you, comrade?

LIBBY. She's been like this for the last few hours. It's the pills.

PETER. Yes –

LIBBY. She's getting very distressed. Confused.

PETER. Let's just –

LIBBY. We gave her the right dose.

PETER. Why don't we…? There.

PETER *takes her pulse.*

And, erm… how are you?

LIBBY. Me?

PETER. Yes. Are you…?

There's a bit of a silence.

LIBBY. I'm tired.

PETER. Right.

More tense silence.

LIBBY. And you? How are you? How are things at home?

PETER. I'm – Actually, I'm doing very well. We're working hard. Trying to rebuild trust – And I have – Lately – I have to say, I have discovered a side of my wife, which is –

Beat.

I have the greatest admiration for her, actually. As a person. Her strength. Her kindness. Her incredible capacity for forgiveness –

Silence.

Do you, by any chance, still have them?

LIBBY. What?

PETER. The pills.

LIBBY *sets off inside the house.*

Can you hear me, Judy?

JUDY. I have signed this house over to my daughter. Everything. It's all hers now. She – Everything.

PETER. Judy?

JUDY. It's her house. She is in complete control.

JUDY *looks at him.*

You're here?

PETER. Yes. Hello. Long time no see.

JUDY. I'm not well.

PETER. No.

JUDY. Mr Peshani –

PETER. Mr Peshani didn't spot it, I'm afraid.

JUDY. It spread.

PETER *nods. He produces a blood-pressure kit. Looks out across the view.*

PETER. I've missed this. This makes you feel better, doesn't it? Looking at this? It doesn't matter what time of the year it is, it's always perfect –

He attaches the cuff to JUDY'S *arm. Silence.*

JUDY. My mother –

PETER. Yes – ?

JUDY. She was a snob.

PETER. Yes. Yes, I know –

JUDY. She would rather – have died – than let the local doctor touch her –

PETER. Would she indeed?

JUDY. She could suss people out – in an instant. Who they were – What they wanted –

Silence. She looks at him.

I wish she had met you.

Uncomfortable little beat. PETER *removes the cuff.*

PETER. Well, your blood pressure's fine.

LIBBY *reappears. She has a bottle of pills.* PETER *gets up and walks to the edge of the garden.*

LIBBY. Here they are. She's had three.

PETER *looks at the box. He takes a prescription pad out of his bag and starts writing.*

PETER. We can, erm – Alright – I'm going to give you something else.

LIBBY *turns (off* PETER*'s expression) to see that* DANIEL *has come out after her and is standing – almost like he's keeping guard. She glances at* PETER, *then –*

LIBBY. Daniel, I wonder if you'd mind –

She gestures to JUDY.

I'm worried that it's going to start raining.

DANIEL *doesn't move, reluctant to leave them.*

Please. I'd be so grateful.

Beat, then DANIEL *goes to* JUDY *and, with great tenderness, scoops her up to carry her inside.*

JUDY. What?

DANIEL (*softly*). It's alright, Jude. It's alright.

JUDY (*terrified*). NO –

DANIEL. It's alright.

He carries her into the house. Beat. PETER *tears off a prescription.*

PETER. Here. Give her these – Discontinue the others, she'll – She'll be fine in a few hours.

LIBBY. Really?

PETER. As good as new.

I think – From now on – Janet doesn't know I've come here today, and I think in the future, it would be better if you saw another doctor.

LIBBY. It wasn't me who told her, you know? I just – I think you should know that.

PETER. I know.

LIBBY. Only last time –

PETER. I know. I was angry.

LIBBY. This is a small town.

PETER. Yes.

LIBBY. Anyone could have done it.

PETER. Well. Not anyone.

LIBBY. You know?

PETER. I think I do.

LIBBY. Who?

PETER. It doesn't matter.

LIBBY. Yes, it does.

PETER. Someone with a – twisted, rather creepy – someone
with a crush on you.

LIBBY. What?

PETER. Oh, come off it, Libby. Didn't you notice? When I
arrived? I questioned him about his swimming?

LIBBY. Daniel?

PETER. He stood there, bold as brass, and told me that it was
going well.

LIBBY. It is. He's had a wonderful season.

Beat.

PETER. It doesn't matter.

LIBBY. What? You think that Daniel – ?

PETER. He left the team, Libby. Months ago. You forget, his
mother is my patient. And yet, here he is. Day in day out.
Still training. Telling you a load of rubbish about winning.
Why do you think that is? It's a schoolboy crush.

Beat.

You remember how he was with all that ridiculous spying?
Creeping around? And obviously, he's – It's destructive –
Well, this is the trouble with that kind of background.

Little silence.

Anyway.

LIBBY. Listen. Peter. What if – Mother might want to see you
again – Please. I wouldn't – I'd stay out of the way. I promise.
I'd go out if necessary. Just – Can we? If she asks for you.

Little silence, then –

PETER. I've already broken a promise to my wife by coming here today. I think – I think I've done enough.

LIBBY. But. Listen – Please.

He stops. Turns. Beat.

I don't want to beg.

She smiles. Beat.

PETER. Then don't.

He goes. LIBBY *crumples. After a few seconds,* DANIEL *appears.*

DANIEL. You okay?

LIBBY *keeps her back to him, tries to regain control of herself.*

LIBBY. Yes. Just… I'm fine. I…

Beat.

DANIEL. Is there anything I can get you?

LIBBY. No. Please. Would you just – could you please leave me alone? I'm sorry –

Silence. DANIEL *moves closer.*

Daniel, Peter has made some – There have been some accusations. Some – actually, some very serious accusations.

DANIEL. What?

LIBBY. About –

She starts to cry again.

DANIEL. Please. Let me get you something –

LIBBY. No. I – Have you quit the team?

Little silence. DANIEL *nods…*

Well, it was very – You were dishonest, actually – Not to –

DANIEL. My mum can't hardly move. I have to turn her. When I'm out she has to lie still. For hours. In the same position.

Beat.

LIBBY. Well. You could have – Why didn't you tell us?

DANIEL. I thought – I wanted to still keep coming here.

LIBBY *nods. Little silence.*

Did he say anything else?

LIBBY. It doesn't matter –

Beat.

I just – In future, I would prefer it if you were honest with me –

DANIEL. I would never –

Beat.

I want you to know that I would never do anything that – I wouldn't. I'd never hurt you.

LIBBY *nods. She's crying again. She tries to control it but she can't.* DANIEL *comes over and puts his hands on her shoulders.*

LIBBY. No –

DANIEL. Sssh – It's alright –

He turns her and takes her gently in his arms. She continues to cry. After a moment she looks up.

I think you're incredible – I – So beautiful –

They face each other for a moment and then, somehow, start to kiss. As they do so, SUMMER *appears at the top of the garden, carrying a suitcase. She's dressed much more smartly than before. She stares at* DANIEL *and* LIBBY *kissing. The lights snap to black.*

Scene Five

House. Evening. LIBBY, NICK, JUDY *and* SUMMER *are sitting at the table. Their meal is over. There are lots of empty bottles.* SUMMER *is talking. She directs almost all her answers to* JUDY *and* NICK.

SUMMER. Everything is in very pale, washed-out colours – Her inspirations were the ocean and the architecture of Cuba. And there are scented candles in all the guest rooms. Mine was mandarin. Oh, and one of the other things Mary collects is antique fans. She's arranged them in groups along the walls.

LIBBY. Seems funny her having a name like Mary.

SUMMER. Why?

LIBBY. Well, it's not very Malaysian, is it?

SUMMER. Western names are actually very common in Malaysia. Anyway, she's got a Malaysian name. She just doesn't use it.

JUDY. What a pity.

SUMMER. In the evening, if you want dinner on the terrace, Dad just switches the speakers through and there's music playing. The speakers are designed to look like part of the building. Everything's remote-controlled. It looks old, but it's actually modern.

NICK. How wonderful.

SUMMER. They do something every weekend. They never just sit around. Sometimes their friends come over for a pool party or a barbecue. Or they have to entertain a business contact from somewhere. And on my last night – we went to Paris.

LIBBY. Oh, Summer!

JUDY. That's wonderful. Did you see the galleries?

SUMMER. No. Dad took us to a laser show.

She takes some more wine.

JUDY. And was he – ?

SUMMER. Oh my God. We had so much in common. We totally like the same food. We both absolutely hate classical music.

LIBBY. You don't hate classical music, Summer.

SUMMER. Yes, I do.

JUDY. What does he look like?

SUMMER. He's – old, but – He looks a bit like me.

NICK. And Mary?

SUMMER. She's extremely attractive. Dad has this home office, which looks like it's old because it's panelled. But you can slide the panels along and there's all these screens in there, like TV screens and projection screens to play games on. Mary never goes in.

JUDY. Why not?

SUMMER. Because it's a boys' room. Mary says that girls should never interrupt boys when they're playing games.

NICK. Mary sounds like a scream.

SUMMER. Except to clean it.

LIBBY. Oh, of course.

SUMMER. Everything is clean there. Everything. She keeps an immaculate house.

LIBBY. I expect she has help.

SUMMER. No. It's a cultural difference. A Malaysian woman would rather die than live in squalor or disgrace her family.

NICK. Do you think you should try Daniel again, Libby?

LIBBY. No. I'm sure he's –

JUDY. Nicky's right. It's so unlike him.

LIBBY. Listen. Summer. I'll tell you what you missed here. Judy had a terrible scare with her pills, didn't you, Mum?

JUDY. Oh, yes, it was frightful.

LIBBY. She was like a zombie. Honestly –

JUDY. I couldn't see anything. It was – Oh God – It was like I was in the back of this cave, or something – and all the voices were terribly remote.

SUMMER. I thought you were better.

JUDY. Oh, I am.

LIBBY. She's fine, darling.

JUDY. There's nothing to worry about.

NICK. I'm going to phone him, Libby.

LIBBY. No, just – And will you be seeing him again?

SUMMER. Of course I will.

LIBBY. Well, that's – When? Soon?

NICK *stands*.

Where are you going?

NICK. What?

LIBBY. I just – I don't think you need any more to drink, that's all. Sit down.

NICK. Don't order me around please, Libby.

LIBBY. We had an agreement. Didn't we? For Summer's party.

NICK. I'm going to call Daniel. Alright?

JUDY. Oh yes –

NICK. I'm extremely worried.

LIBBY. I – What is the matter with you? I rang Daniel.

NICK. Yes, but you didn't speak to him.

LIBBY. I left a message. Why must you always – ? Summer is trying to tell us all about her holiday in France.

SUMMER. It's alright. I've finished now.

LIBBY. Well. I may have some – There are still some questions I'd like to ask, actually.

SUMMER. Mum, why don't you just stop pissing around and tell them –

Little beat.

LIBBY. What?

SUMMER. She knows where Daniel is.

LIBBY. What are you talking about? No, I don't.

SUMMER. Yes, you do. Tell them.

JUDY. Summer, what do you mean?

NICK. I'm sorry. Does she know or doesn't she?

SUMMER *stares at* LIBBY. *Waiting.*

SUMMER. Right. That's a shame.

JUDY. Summer, darling. I don't understand.

SUMMER. I really hoped you'd do the right thing for once –

NICK. Does anyone else feel slightly scared?

SUMMER. So. I'm going to have to take over. As usual.

LIBBY. Summer, just stop it.

SUMMER. I know where Daniel is. He's throwing up somewhere.

JUDY. What?

SUMMER. He's disgusted. By what happened to him, here. This afternoon.

Little silence.

NICK. I'm sorry – what is she saying?

SUMMER. She snogged him. I walked in and saw her. She may have been doing it for months for all I know.

JUDY. What?

SUMMER. She was snogging him – here – when I came into the garden –

NICK. Oh my God.

JUDY. Libby?

SUMMER. She can't control herself.

JUDY. Libby, is this true?

LIBBY. Don't question me.

NICK. Daniel?

SUMMER. Yep.

NICK. Daniel and Libby?

LIBBY. And I have told you, Summer, about sneaking around.

SUMMER. Excuse me –

LIBBY. That was – sit down, Summer. I want you to understand. That was not –

SUMMER. What?

LIBBY. It was – actually – very different – to what you're thinking –

SUMMER. Oh. I'm sorry. What were you actually doing then?

LIBBY. Listen –

SUMMER. Judo?

JUDY. Summer, please. Let me say something –

SUMMER. You made me a promise. You lied to me. Again.

LIBBY. No, wait –

SUMMER. You're a liar. You're – Jesus – everything about you makes me sick.

LIBBY. Calm down.

NICK. Why should she? She's absolutely right.

LIBBY. Shut up, Nick.

JUDY. Summer, darling. Listen to me –

SUMMER. No.

JUDY. Listen to me, please, if you won't listen to your mum –

SUMMER. She made me a promise.

LIBBY. Summer, please –

JUDY. And she kept it, darling –

LIBBY. Yes – I did.

SUMMER. Are you kidding me?

JUDY. No –

SUMMER. She snogged the fucking pool boy!

JUDY. Yes. But with Peter, Summer – That was the promise – With Peter – And she ended that.

Little beat.

SUMMER. What?

JUDY. It ended, darling.

LIBBY. Mum –

JUDY. Long before you got back.

LIBBY. No –

JUDY. And, yes. She suffered terribly when Peter's wife found out, but –

SUMMER. Peter? Peter's wife?

NICK. Summer, what exactly did you see?

LIBBY. Stay out of this please, Nick?

NICK. Was she touching him?

SUMMER. Yes.

NICK. Groping him?

SUMMER. She was like a fucking rapist.

JUDY. Don't use those harsh words, Summer.

SUMMER. Ah, yeah. I get it. He was – She got dumped by Peter so she – Just to make herself feel like she was worth something, she – Yeah. She threw herself at someone else.

LIBBY. Summer –

SUMMER. Like a desperate slag. You did that before, didn't you, Mum? Back in Spain. Do you remember? He was going to be the answer to all our problems – Roy.

Beat.

Do you know what you are, Mum? You're actually –

SUMMER *leaves*. LIBBY *follows*.

LIBBY. Summer!

JUDY. Summer, darling –

NICK. I'm not staying here.

JUDY. Nicky –

NICK. I'm not. I'm leaving. She knew exactly how I felt about him. I have to go.

JUDY. Nick. Please. Listen – Listen to me.

LIBBY *appears*.

LIBBY. She's run off.

JUDY. Libby, why didn't you tell me?

LIBBY. Not now, Mum.

JUDY. I would have helped you. I would have guided you both.

NICK. I want to know how long it went on for.

JUDY. Nick, let me finish.

LIBBY. It didn't 'go on'. It was a stupid –

NICK. Weeks? Months?

LIBBY. Once. A one-off.

JUDY. But if he loves you –

LIBBY. Oh, Mum, for Christ's sake – forget that. It's Summer – That's all I care about.

> LIBBY *sits down. Beat.*

NICK. You have a very nasty streak in you, Libby.

LIBBY. We're going to have to go.

JUDY. What?

LIBBY. In the morning. I'll take her away.

JUDY. Oh, Libby, no.

LIBBY. I owe her that much. She needs a home. I should never have brought her here in the first place.

NICK. Don't worry – I'm going too.

JUDY. No, please. Both of you –

NICK. I actually think – the time has come – for you – Libby – to think about some kind of professional psychiatric help. I think that you may have been warped somehow –

LIBBY. Shut up, Nick.

NICK. By some kind of a – No, I'm serious – / an issue in your past –

LIBBY. Do you want to start lecturing / me?

NICK. Yes –

LIBBY. About my psychological health –

JUDY. That's enough.

NICK. I have had my demons, Libby –

LIBBY. Ha!

NICK. And I have faced them –

LIBBY. You've *what*?

NICK. What is it do you think that compels you – I am trying to understand here / to destroy the happiness –

LIBBY. Are you insane?

NICK. It's jealousy!

LIBBY. What?

NICK. You hate me –

LIBBY. / You're drunk –

NICK. You want to see me suffer –

LIBBY. / This is –

NICK. Because you hate me –

LIBBY. / As usual – Bullshit – theatrics –

NICK. I loved him – ! I felt something very real – I did – I may have run away from it. I may have – Yes. I was afraid – but you took that away from me – you couldn't bear to see it.

JUDY. Right. I want you both to calm down.

NICK. I am finally coming out about this, Libby – Finally – After all these years. All these years that you have made me feel worthless. Scared of you.

LIBBY. I made you feel – ?

NICK. My feelings – Yes – were never considered.

LIBBY. Your feelings?

JUDY. Right. Now I want you both to listen to me.

LIBBY (*to* NICK). When I think of what I have been through with you –

JUDY. Oh, for God's sake –

LIBBY. *Your feelings?*

JUDY. What does any of this matter?

LIBBY. I have – Oh my God – Years of it, Nick.

JUDY. Stop! / STOP.

LIBBY. Finding you. Losing you. Phone calls about you.

NICK. Oh, yes –

LIBBY. You're in a toilet, passed out. You're – They've found you with a bit of tube wrapped round your arm in a fucking toilet – a toilet in a fucking station. You've – someone's beaten you up. You've been arrested. You owe money. You shit yourself in a pub. Someone's – a friend of yours has gone blind –

Beat.

NICK. Those were instances –

LIBBY. You've had a prolapse – Your veins collapsing. Your heart –

NICK. And it is in very poor taste to rake up past episodes –

LIBBY. Your fucking feelings, Nick – or your attempts to blot them out at any rate –

NICK. / I cleaned up –

LIBBY. – have dominated – I mean that – dominated the whole of my adult life.

Silence.

I look at myself and I see – Yes – exactly what Summer sees. I am – angry. Pathetic – She's right. Dead right. I hear myself – my voice – and I think – who is that speaking? Telling everybody – Ordering everybody around? And even when something nice is happening or everybody's having fun, I try to sound laid-back or – like I'm in the spirit of it, but – it's fake. I copy.

Beat.

I'm actually – What I'm actually doing is this – like this –

She makes a ball with her interlocked fists.

I can't sleep. On car journeys. In case the driver –

She turns to NICK.

But you –

Then JUDY.

And you –

She swings back round to NICK.

You're empty, Nick. There's nothing inside you. You're hollow. You're screaming for attention but you have no strength. No wonder Grandpa despised you. Filling up that space – that gap – with drugs – I despise you.

Little pause.

NICK. I think we ought to talk about this house.

Little beat. LIBBY *looks at him with absolute disgust.*

LIBBY. You really are –

NICK. Just tell her. While we're all getting things off our chests. Tell her.

JUDY. Tell me what?

LIBBY. I'm tired.

JUDY. We're all tired.

NICK. Tell her. You think you can talk about my mistakes –

LIBBY. You tell her.

Beat.

JUDY. I want to know what's going on –

Little beat.

NICK. This house –

JUDY. Yes – ?

NICK. This land –

JUDY. Yes. What? Spit it out.

NICK. It's – Everything we own, everything – is on a long and very elaborate loan.

Beat.

JUDY. What are you talking about?

NICK. We're on borrowed time, Mummy, darling. We're tenants. Your daughter – Yes? The one you thought was so responsible –

LIBBY. You can't even get this right –

NICK. Shut up.

LIBBY. That's not how it works –

NICK. I thought your energy was failing.

LIBBY. Listen – I did a very stupid thing. Alright? I fucked up.

JUDY. I wish one of you would start making sense.

LIBBY. I got myself involved in – something – Looking back on it –

NICK. Oh, here we go –

LIBBY. No –

NICK. Rewriting history.

LIBBY. I was manipulated –

NICK. What?

LIBBY. To a certain extent.

JUDY. What's happened? For Christ's sake. Just tell me. Straight.

Little beat.

LIBBY. It's called equity release. It's nothing sinister. It's a way of raising capital, that's all.

Beat.

You have an asset – a house –

NICK. This house.

LIBBY. And you release the value of that asset. You – You get the cash –

NICK. By selling it.

LIBBY. Shut up. You sell it. Yes. Effectively. But you retain the right to – We're not tenants. We're not. We have full rights of residency.

NICK (*to* JUDY). Until you die.

LIBBY. Yes. And then –

Little beat.

JUDY. But what will you do?

LIBBY. We'll be fine.

JUDY. This house was for you.

LIBBY. Yes. Well, I've fucked that up, haven't I, Mum? I've made a fuck-up of that.

Beat.

But I had no help. No support. I was completely alone.

Little silence.

JUDY. Did you get a lot of money for it?

Beat. NICK *starts to laugh quietly, bitterly.*

LIBBY. There were a lot of debts against it. They had to be taken into account. And then there was the condition – that was a significant factor – the condition of the place.

NICK. She gave it away, basically.

LIBBY. There's a few thousand. We're not completely bereft.

Silence.

There's still one or two of those watercolours – they're quite valuable. And the Staffordshire figures.

JUDY. Why, Libby?

LIBBY. I thought I was in love.

Beat.

I think – Looking back on it – I think he probably had
something like this in mind from – Yes – I was extremely
stupid.

JUDY. I don't understand.

Little beat.

You don't mean – ?

LIBBY. Peter.

Silence.

NICK. She thought he was going to take her in –

LIBBY. Alright, Nick.

NICK. She thought they were going to live here – together –
happily – like two – The doctor and his second wife.

Silence. JUDY *then – suddenly, unexpectedly – she begins to
ROAR with laughter.*

JUDY. I'm sorry –

NICK. You think it's funny – ?

JUDY. I do – I'm sorry – Oh my God –

She tries to control herself but she's off again.

I'm sorry – Oh my God – Well. They're much more the type,
really – aren't they? To live in a house like this. What was
the wife called – ?

LIBBY. Janet.

JUDY. Yes. She'll have the place shipshape in no time, just you
wait. Janet. Little bowls of peonies, hyacinths. She'll have
her antique fans up on the wall – Yes – And Peter. Much
more the type.

NICK. I don't believe you.

JUDY. Take my advice, will you? Go away, my darlings. Go far away. And don't weigh yourself down with possessions – travel light. Eat off paper plates – I mean it. Go. Be free.

JUDY laughs again. There's a long silence.

NICK. If somebody has strong feelings for someone –

JUDY. Oh, Nicky –

NICK. Then that person should be considered out of bounds.

JUDY. Nicky, please. I think you should probably – I'm not going to last much longer – I think it's time you started to grow up.

Little beat. NICK *looks aghast.*

NICK. What?

JUDY. And you, Libby. Neither of you is very – It's my fault, I know that.

NICK. I can't believe –

JUDY. But since I have this – very little time –

NICK. Is this a joke?

JUDY. Try not to be angry, darling. Try to listen.

LIBBY. I think she's right.

NICK. What?

LIBBY. I think we all need to start living in the real world.

NICK. Well, that's a fairly new development, wouldn't you say?

JUDY. No. Listen –

NICK. Tell me. Tell me about the real world, Mother, darling. I'm fascinated to know. When would you say you first discovered it?

LIBBY. Nick –

NICK. When you were playing Hindu holy men with all the other brats?

JUDY. Listen –

NICK. We lived in the real world, Mum. Me and Libby. We lived here. With your fucking parents. Didn't we?

JUDY. I know you did.

NICK. And there was nothing more real – nothing – than your fucking – vicious – fucking father.

JUDY. Alright.

NICK. Don't you dare talk to me about the real world.

Little beat.

JUDY. I did what I thought was best.

NICK. Oh, please.

JUDY. For you. I did. I made mistakes. Let's not rake it all up again.

LIBBY. What do you mean, again?

NICK. We liked India.

JUDY. Libby didn't.

NICK. I did. I liked it. Why didn't you get rid of her if she was so unhappy? I would have stayed. I wanted to stay. Libby, tell her. Tell her what it was like.

LIBBY. You don't need my help.

NICK. It was – And the cause! That's what's so hilarious. The great fucking cause that you were fighting for –

JUDY. No –

NICK. Your shining cause –

JUDY. I won't – No, Nicky – I won't apologise for that.

NICK. Why not?

JUDY. Because that – I believed – I still believe – was very important.

NICK. Are you getting this? I'll tell you about your cause, Mum –

JUDY. We were trying to / change an unjust society –

NICK. Oh, I know. I know you were. And let's just – Do you mind if I do a quick assessment – ?

JUDY. You cannot possibly quantify –

NICK. Oh? Don't you think so? I think when something is so important that you'd give up your children for it –

JUDY. Nicky –

NICK. We can be permitted a little stocktake, can't we?

JUDY. You're angry, Nick, but you're not listening.

NICK. No sign of peace or equality, I'm afraid. No justice. But, hang on a minute! Henna tattoos are still making an impact, so – Yoga – Yeah, that's something – Wholemeal bread.

Beat.

And the drugs, of course – Oh and what's this? Steeleye Span are still touring the globe? Well, that's a comfort, isn't it? At least your revolution wasn't entirely in vain.

JUDY. You're actually revealing a great deal about yourself –

NICK. I don't know if you noticed, Mum. But while you were wanking into a chrysanthemum, Margaret Thatcher was making her entrance. Did you see? Jesse Helms. Ronald Reagan. Now that was a revolution. They knew the terrain, darling – scorched earth. Jesus Christ – You hippies – you could have learned a thing or two about changing the world from those people.

He swigs gin. Little silence.

JUDY. Well.

Silence.

I suppose that's all true, isn't it?

Silence.

A Quaker came to the house once – I lived in a squat in Belsize Park – and he came to talk to us. We were a peace group. We gave him a meal. And after dinner – he said that

within every one of us there was a light. And that the more
we lived – the more fully – the more we gave of ourselves –
the brighter it would shine. I was young. Twenty. And if the
lights could join together – if they could join up to become a
great brightness – I gave out food in those days. We called it
Social Action. I gave out food and clothes – the housewives
used to laugh at the way I spoke, but they were never unkind.
Sometimes we were hungry ourselves. Often.

Beat.

I've seen riots. I've hurled paving stones at policemen. I've
drunk. I've smoked. Wonderful things have happened to me
– I've fired a gun.

Beat.

I've kept the light – here – alive. I've kept it burning. And I
apologise for nothing.

Little silence.

'Wanking into a chrysanthemum.' You could have done
wonderful things with your ability to speak.

NICK. Yeah, well.

JUDY. Instead, you wasted it.

Little silence.

LIBBY. I've nursed three people in this house. I've just
realised. Three deathbeds. Granny, Grandpa and now you.

SUMMER. Has the shouting stopped?

They turn round to see SUMMER *standing.*

LIBBY. Summer –

JUDY. Summer, darling –

LIBBY. Summer, I am really sorry.

SUMMER. It's alright.

LIBBY. No. I mean it.

SUMMER. I've told you. It's alright. Actually – I'm sorry.

LIBBY. No –

SUMMER. I am. I shouldn't have – You're alright, really.

LIBBY. Listen. I want you and me to go away somewhere, alright? And I don't mean that fucking place in Spain. A really brilliant place. For us. I want us to settle down and start completely from scratch. I'm not working in any more seasonal –

SUMMER. No –

LIBBY. I'm not. I'm going to use my brain –

SUMMER. I want to live with my dad.

Little silence.

LIBBY. What?

SUMMER. In France.

Beat.

LIBBY. Summer, sweetheart –

SUMMER. You'd get on so much better on your own, Mum –

LIBBY. No. No, I wouldn't. No.

SUMMER. Just listen. You could – You'd have a bit of freedom. You deserve that. You've looked after other people for your whole life.

LIBBY. No.

SUMMER. And you could – Yeah. You could go back to Spain, or –

LIBBY. Summer. Listen –

SUMMER. Enjoy yourself.

Little beat.

LIBBY. Listen. Sweetheart. I know you had a lovely time there, but – It's one thing to have a holiday. I mean, of course they fell in love with you, darling. Of course they did. But – Your dad and Mary might not want –

SUMMER. It was his idea.

Little silence.

LIBBY. Oh.

Another beat.

SUMMER. There's a very good school nearby. I think it would be a really good idea.

Beat.

I do. I think it would be a good idea, Mum. For both of us.

LIBBY. Well, perhaps we should talk about it in the morning.

Beat. SUMMER *nods.*

SUMMER. Just think of all the things you could do if you were free to move around.

LIBBY. We'll talk about it in the morning.

Another little silence.

SUMMER. Goodnight, then.

JUDY. Goodnight, darling.

SUMMER *goes, then turns.*

SUMMER. Don't stay up too late.

SUMMER *goes. Silence.* LIBBY *starts to clear the debris from the table.*

JUDY. Libby –

LIBBY. I want to get this all cleared up. I hate coming down to it.

She carries on in silence. After a little while, she just grinds to a halt.

JUDY. She might feel differently tomorrow.

NICK. Yeah.

LIBBY. Oh, I'm sure she will. She's famous for it. You remember the trouble I had trying to get her to go there in the first place? She's always doing this. I don't know what's the matter with her.

Silence. LIBBY *just stands there.*

JUDY. Neither of you – no matter what you've done – has made as many terrible mistakes as I have.

Beat.

I have been –

LIBBY. It's very hard to be a parent.

Silence. JUDY *nods.*

JUDY. Come and sit down, Libby.

LIBBY *starts clearing again.*

Please.

She stops, but doesn't move.

Come and sit here with me. And you, Nicky. Please. Just for a moment.

NICK *comes over to* JUDY.

Libby?

Finally, LIBBY *comes over and sits down.*

NICK. What are you going to do? Sing to us?

JUDY. I just thought it would be nice to all – sit together. Just for a moment. I know we haven't had very many moments like this and that's – Well. Obviously that's my fault. I haven't given you very – quiet lives.

Little beat.

But perhaps we could all – just –

NICK. Pretend?

JUDY. Yes. If you like.

NICK *lays his head in* JUDY*'s lap.*

I want to be able to help you – Even if it's only –

Beat.

I know what I've done. I know that – In the end – it's down to me.

LIBBY. Do you think we could sit in silence?

JUDY. Yes, of course.

Little beat.

NICK. No one's to blame for anyone else's fuck-ups. We all fucked up. We all fucked up our own lives. Nobody made me a junkie. Except possibly David Bowie.

Little silence.

JUDY. Everything will be alright. Human beings are – They're remarkably resilient. That's the wonder of them.

Little beat.

'Lone trees grow strong.' Remember that, Libby. It's a saying. Winston Churchill.

Beat.

NICK. 'If they grow at all.'

JUDY. What?

NICK. 'Lone trees – '

JUDY. Yes –

NICK. 'If they grow at all, grow strong.'

JUDY. That's right. Yes.

She looks at LIBBY*, pulls her in with her arm until her head is resting on* JUDY*'s shoulder.*

That's how it goes. 'If they grow at all.' Yes. Wonderful.

Scene Six

*Garden. It's a bright, sunny, winter's day. Bare trees, big sky.
NICK is standing at the top of the steps. He's wearing a dark
suit with no shirt underneath and his string of pearls roped
around his neck. We can see that, under his shoes, his feet are
bandaged, and he's supporting himself with a rather grotty old
crutch. He looks terrible. At the bottom of the garden, PETER is
standing in a smart suit and tie.*

PETER. Very moving, I thought. And I loved the fusion of – all
the different spiritual elements. Really –

Beat.

Did I spot some of the – ? I thought perhaps there were one
or two –

NICK. Orange people? They'll always come out for a jolly. I
think they were a bit pissed off actually. Thought we should
have set her ablaze and flung her down the Ganges.
However. I suppose we could have tipped her off the back of
the Torpoint Ferry, but one never thinks of these things in
time. Do you have a cigarette?

PETER. No.

Beat.

I spoke to a very interesting lady –

NICK. Was she German?

PETER. No. She had – on her arms –

NICK. Tattoos. Sheila.

PETER. Yes. One of the old guard. Keeps bees now, apparently.

NICK. It's funny, isn't it? They all start off trying to save
humanity. But once they've worked out what an utterly,

fucking, futile enterprise that is, they move on to wildlife. I
can't tell you the number of people I spoke to who now run
donkey sanctuaries.

PETER. I hope Janet and I weren't – We stayed right at the
back. We didn't want to draw attention to ourselves.

NICK. You didn't. We were quite oblivious.

Little silence.

PETER. And the sun came out. That was nice. When we were
crossing the river it was streaming down onto the house, like
– It was beautiful.

NICK. I was going to read a poem.

PETER. Yes?

NICK. It's Indian, of course.

He fishes a ragged scrap of paper out.

'Things that I longed for in vain and things that I got – let
them pass.'

He stands looking at the page for quite a long time.

'Let me but truly possess the things that I ever spurned – and
overlooked.'

Long pause. Finally he looks up.

Nice, isn't it?

PETER. It's beautiful.

Beat.

NICK. Well. Anyway. I didn't read it. I'm no good, really, with
people staring at me.

Little pause.

Quite a good turn-out actually.

PETER. Yes.

NICK. Considering. That's how it must be at the funerals of fighter pilots. Wobbly war heroes – each time a few less.

Beat.

You really ought to have spoken to that German woman. She was a scream. Psychotherapist, apparently. Did you see her when they wheeled old Judy into the oven – ?

PETER. Yes –

NICK. She –

He puts his fist up in a salute.

Mum would have shrieked.

He hobbles towards the house.

PETER. Did you have an accident?

NICK *stops.*

The crutch. I thought you might have –

NICK. Oh. That. No. I'm surprised you haven't come across this before, Peter. What with you being a doctor and all.

PETER. Oh.

NICK. Yes. Booze. The reaping of what one sows. The reckoning. Funny really. I appear to be dying as I've lived. Feet first.

LIBBY *comes out of the house carrying a cardboard box. She's wearing a black suit and dark sunglasses.*

Got any cigarettes?

LIBBY. On the table.

NICK *heads indoors.*

There's plenty to do in there. You can bring some boxes down.

NICK. I don't know if I've got the strength for the stairs, Lib.

LIBBY. Find it. And bring the parcel tape when you come.

He goes. LIBBY *busies herself packing books from the solarium.* PETER *watches.*

PETER. I was saying to Nick. I thought the service was very moving.

Janet and I kept very much in the background. We didn't want to –

Beat.

But it was very important for me to pay my respects – I hope you, erm – She was an extraordinary lady. Tremendous courage.

LIBBY. She died like anybody else dies. You've seen death.

PETER. Yes.

LIBBY. My grandparents both went the same way. When people say, 'She died bravely,' they mean, quietly. Without a fuss. She died without screaming the bloody house down. Well – is that courage? It's tasteful, I suppose. Have you seen a roll of bubble wrap?

PETER *crosses to a chair where there is a roll of old bubble wrap.* LIBBY *comes down to collect it from him.*

PETER. Libby –

But she takes the roll and walks away immediately.

Couldn't you just stop for a second?

LIBBY. I'm sorry, Peter, but we're moving house. There's an awful lot of work involved.

PETER. I just want to talk to you.

LIBBY. So, talk. We've got until this evening, I assume?

PETER. What?

LIBBY. Before we have to go.

PETER. Oh. I don't think there's any particular –

LIBBY. Good. We're only taking what we can carry anyway.

She crosses and begins packing boxes.

PETER. I have the most tremendous memories of this house. Of this family. Of you –

LIBBY. You'll need to get the piano tuned.

PETER. What?

LIBBY. There's a man in Totnes. Only, I have a feeling he went to prison.

PETER. Libby, please – I want to just –

LIBBY carries on. PETER moves closer to her.

I loved your mother.

Beat.

And you. I did. I loved you.

Little beat. LIBBY stops working.

I never want you to think that there wasn't real – That my feelings were ever – I fell into a terrible decline when I heard about Judy. I did. It was – I had this depression, this feeling in the pit of my stomach. It was terrible. I felt – bereft.

Beat.

I thought, that's it. There's no one left like that. With that passion, those beliefs. It's the end of something. I pulled the car over and I wept. I carried it around with me for days. I'm still carrying it. And there was no one I could talk to. Janet –

Beat.

Janet, let's just say, has found a way of turning forgiveness into a new and perpetual kind of torture –

Little silence. PETER reaches out and touches LIBBY's shoulder. They stand still for a second, then LIBBY moves away from PETER and into the solarium.

Honestly, Libby. If you knew how much I've thought about you. How I've run it – over and over in my mind.

LIBBY *comes out of the solarium with a small bag.*

The things I should have said. The things I want to say.

LIBBY *spreads the contents in a huge powdery arc across the flower beds. An enormous amount of the contents land on* PETER. *It's* JUDY*'s ashes.*

Jesus Christ, Libby! Oh my God! What are you – ? Is that – ?

LIBBY. The last of the Haussmans. Interred in her own garden. As requested. You ought to dig that in. You'll get lovely hydrangeas.

NICK *comes out of the house.*

NICK. Is this parcel tape?

LIBBY. No, Nick. It's ribbon.

NICK. You see how my aesthetic sense still dominates? How long have we got before the new masters come clattering up the drive?

LIBBY. We'll be gone by tonight, is that alright, Peter?

PETER. You can have as long as you need.

LIBBY. How very generous. Did you hear that, Nick?

NICK. Yes.

LIBBY. And isn't it generous?

NICK. I'm weeping on the inside.

NICK *sets off for the house again.*

PETER. Well, I suppose I'll go then.

LIBBY. Please thank Janet for coming to the funeral.

PETER *nods.*

I think everyone was very impressed.

PETER *looks at her for a moment and then walks away. There is a beat as* LIBBY *watches him go.*

NICK (*off*). Guess what I've found.

LIBBY *ignores him.*

There's an entire drinks cabinet in here that I didn't know existed. I can hear the bottles rattling. I'm going to try and force the door.

LIBBY. Don't be ridiculous.

NICK (*off*). What?

LIBBY. Don't be ridiculous!

NICK *appears. He's carrying a posy of flowers.*

NICK. I'm not leaving it for them. What about the flowers?

LIBBY. We'll run them down to the hospital.

NICK. This one's from Summer.

LIBBY. Well, that one's very pretty, isn't it.

She touches the petals.

We'll keep that one.

NICK. Do you know what flashed into my head this morning? Those access visits. Do you remember? With Granny. She used to take us out to meet her.

LIBBY. Oh my God.

NICK. Remember?

LIBBY. Grandpa wouldn't have her in the house.

NICK. Exactly. And she was so weird. She was strung out. I hated it.

LIBBY. What about the vagrant years?

NICK. Oh Christ.

LIBBY. When she turned up at that café like a tramp.

NICK. In some weird coat.

LIBBY (*continued*). And she had streaks of shit all down her tights.

NICK (*continued*). Where the fuck had she been?

LIBBY. Remember Granny?

NICK (*upper-class accent*). 'We can never go back to that Wimpy.'

They laugh. He goes inside.

LIBBY. I keep remembering a story about India. Do you remember that little van she used to drive out there? There was a little yellow van with birds on it – you don't remember, you were too young. One time, she was on the rice run or something, and she took you along with her – You must have been about two. And, of course, she was in a state of fucking grace as usual, singing away – And there was no passenger door on the van, and almost certainly no seatbelt – And as she took a particularly sharp corner, you toppled out of the van and rolled into a ditch.

Beat.

She didn't notice until she got to Poona. She was too blissed out. If you hadn't been found by the kulfi man you might have been raised by wolves.

Beat.

I don't know why that came into my head this morning –

Silence.

It really made me laugh.

NICK (*off*). I can't hear a word you're saying.

We hear the sound of wood cracking.

LIBBY. Nick, just leave it. Anyway, you promised me you were going on to beer. For your health.

DANIEL. Sounds like an interesting conversation.

LIBBY *spins round to see* DANIEL. *He looks older. Not in years but in confidence and manner. He's wearing a suit and is quite tanned.*

LIBBY. Oh my God.

DANIEL. Hello.

LIBBY. Daniel! I don't believe it. Were you at the funeral? I didn't see you.

DANIEL. I was at the back. To one side. It doesn't matter.

LIBBY. No, but I would have liked to. Gosh, you look well. Where have you been?

DANIEL. Australia.

LIBBY. Australia?

DANIEL. And China. Greece. Singapore.

LIBBY. I don't believe it.

DANIEL. And Çanakkale.

LIBBY. Çanakkale?

DANIEL. It's in Turkey. They host the Baltic Swimming Federation.

LIBBY. You're swimming.

DANIEL. I've been everywhere, really. Argentina.

LIBBY. Argentina!

DANIEL. Everywhere.

Little silence.

LIBBY. And how's your mum?

DANIEL. She's okay. She's – They want her to have an operation, so – she's trying to lose some of the weight. My dad came back.

LIBBY. He did?

DANIEL. Not to stay. Just – He got her a carer.

LIBBY. I can't get used to you in that suit. I'm sorry.

DANIEL. It's only Burton's.

LIBBY. Still. So smart.

DANIEL. I wanted to say something. It's – The thing is – I'm sorry for running away like that.

LIBBY. No, Daniel, please.

DANIEL. It was wrong. I should have –

LIBBY. No. If anyone should be sorry, it's me.

DANIEL. No. I don't want you to apologise for that. I don't want you to regret it. Ever. I don't.

Silence.

I feel like I should – I got so much from you. From Judy. I shouldn't have gone without – I should have said thank you.

LIBBY. It wasn't necessary.

DANIEL. Yeah, but I never did. To Judy. I never told her –

LIBBY. Daniel – She knew. Of course she knew.

DANIEL *nods. A silence.*

DANIEL. Sometimes when I'm going somewhere and I think, oh my God what am I doing here, do you know what I mean? Really nervous, like – It's terrifying, isn't it?

LIBBY. Yes.

DANIEL. Do you know what I mean?

LIBBY. Yes.

DANIEL. And I think, fuck. I can't do this. I can't just walk into a city, and – get a taxi, I can't do it. I can't speak Japanese, or whatever. And then I think, fuck it. Yes I can. Why can't I? I can give it a fucking go, anyway.

Beat.

And that's Judy. She gave me that. That's Judy. Alive in me.

LIBBY. Well. That's a very fitting memorial.

NICK *appears.*

Look who's here.

NICK. Well, well. I thought you'd forgotten our plans to elope.

DANIEL. Never.

LIBBY. He looks well, doesn't he? He's been all around the world.

NICK. Have I got time to throw a few blouses into a bag?

DANIEL. Of course.

NICK. What climate shall I pack for?

DANIEL. Tropical.

He smiles, goes into the solarium, picking up a trowel as he goes.

LIBBY. Leave that cabinet alone.

NICK. Don't you ever get tired of issuing orders, Libby? I would if I were you.

He's gone. A moment.

DANIEL. I'd probably better –

LIBBY. Are you going somewhere else?

DANIEL. South Africa.

LIBBY *laughs a little*.

Can I say something else?

LIBBY. Of course.

DANIEL. You might not like it.

LIBBY. Daniel, I have heard enough things in this garden –

DANIEL. Don't waste your life.

Silence.

You've always been. To me. The most – Incredible – You're like a goddess.

LIBBY. Goodness, Daniel. You are good for the ego.

DANIEL. I want you to understand – that you could – do – absolutely – anything you wanted.

Silence. DANIEL *leaves. Turns.*

Once. We were in Spain. In this hotel. Outside in this courtyard. And we all had to tell the story of our first kiss –

Little beat.

And mine was the best.

DANIEL *leaves.* LIBBY *stands alone in the garden for a moment. We hear a crash from inside the house.*

NICK (*off*). Now we're making some headway!

LIBBY. You can clear that glass away!

NICK (*off*). What?

LIBBY. I said –

LIBBY *stops, looks out across the garden again.*

Let's get out of here soon. Before it's dark. Let's just pick up what we can carry and go –

NICK (*off*). What?

LIBBY. I think we should go!

NICK (*off*). Where? Where are we going to? That's the thing – Orphans of the storm –

LIBBY. I've been thinking about the West of Ireland. Somewhere that suits my mood. Or Greece.

NICK (*off*). Where?

LIBBY. Anywhere – Çanakkale.

She picks up the boxes and heads for the house.

NICK (*off*). There's no dustpan and brush in here.

LIBBY. Yes there is.

NICK (*off*). There's not. There's only the one upstairs.

LIBBY. Look in the larder –

NICK (*off*). What?

LIBBY. There's a blue-handled one in larder. Where all the mops are and everything –

NICK starts hammering into the cocktail cabinet again. Bang, bang. LIBBY pauses for a second on the veranda, then walks into the house. For a moment the stage is empty, just the garden and the house and the sound of NICK smashing the cabinet. The lights begin to fade.

End of play.